A New Meeting of the Religions

A NEW MEETING OF THE RELIGIONS

*Interreligious Relationships
and
Theological Questioning*

E. Luther Copeland

Baylor University Press
Waco, Texas

Copyright © 1999 by
Baylor University Press
Waco, Texas 76798
All Rights Reserved

Library of Congress Cataloging-in-Publication Data
Copeland, E. Luther, 1916-
    A new meeting of the religions : interreligious relationships and theological questioning / E. Luther Copeland.
        p.   cm.
    Includes bibliographical references.
    ISBN 978-1-4813-1109-0 (alk. paper)
    1. Christianity and other religions. 2. Missions--Theory.
I. Title.
BR127.C64 1999
261.2--dc21   99-12735
                                                                     CIP

CONTENTS

PREFACE vii

PART 1–
Introduction, Terminology, and Represenative Viewpoints 1

   1. The New Encounter
      and the Christian Theology of Religions 3

   2. Theology of Religions:
      Representative Viewpoints 23

PART 2–
Theology of Religions and Theological Questions 47

   3. Articulating the Questions 49

   4. The Christian Mission and Other Missions 73

   5. Interreligious Relationships 97

   6. The Redeemed Community,
      In History and Beyond 121

CONCLUSION 143

NOTES 147

BIBLIOGRAPHY 163

INDEX 173

Preface

WHY THIS BOOK—especially since there are many books dealing with the same subject? One answer is that most Christians are concerned with a rationale for supporting Christian missions among international religions and cultures, if they can do so with integrity and with justification for wholehearted respect for the other religions and the cultures informed by them. This book intends to provide just such a rationale, to demonstrate that one can affirm the Christian mission internationally and interculturally without diminishing either the importance of good interreligious relationships or the recognition of the worth of the major religions—though I am not claiming that there are no other volumes that do so.

In recent years, especially in Christian circles, a new discipline has emerged dealing with how the world religions are meeting each other in new ways and called *theology of religions*. This new discipline takes the relation of Christianity to the other religions with great seriousness. Many Christian theologians see this issue of interreligious relationships as the most crucial challenge to Christian theology since the danger and opportunity posed by Darwinism in the nineteenth century. The literature being produced is voluminous indeed.

Therefore, it is certainly appropriate to ask why another book on this subject is needed. A reason more fundamental, though perhaps not more significant, than the one given above is simply that this volume is *unique*. Part One, composed of Chapters One and Two, seeks to lay a foundation for Part Two, in which my own viewpoint is set forth. Chapter One, after discussing several other introductory matters, contributes a critical assessment of the three terms commonly used to express the Christian attitude toward the other religions—*exclusivism, inclusivism* and *pluralism*—finds this terminology wanting, and suggests a new set of categories. In addition, it offers a more comprehensive treatment than usual of the reasons why religious *pluralism* has become so widespread today. Chapter Two briefly discusses some typical Christian theologies of religion, pluralistic and non-pluralistic. Within the limits of this rather sparse sampling, a special effort is made to represent not only the Christian theological spectrum but also Christian theological thinkers from various parts of the globe. For the most part I have allowed these scholars to speak for themselves, reserving any discussion I may have with them for later chapters where I describe my own viewpoint.

Part Two, which includes Chapters Three through Six, is unique in that it attempts to set forth a theology of religions in terms of the great variety of theological questions raised by the new meeting of world religions. First, the questions themselves are identified, and then theological answers are suggested. Though it is likely that a treatment of all these questions may be found scattered throughout the burgeoning literature of a Christian theology of religions, to my knowledge, no one has attempted either to indicate just what these questions are or to discuss all of them. That is precisely what this book attempts to do, though the discussions are more suggestive than comprehensive.

I wish to emphasize that what is discussed in this volume is a *Christian* theology of religions, which concerns itself primarily with the issue of how religions may relate to each other. Of course, representatives of other religions are free to make similar attempts from their own faith perspective, though they may well reject the designation of *theology* as a Christian term.

Likewise, in my judgment, to construct a *Christian world theology* which seeks to take into account the insights of the different religions is invalid if it requires that the theologian step outside the circle of his or her own faith and accept a viewpoint that transcends all claims to religious revelation. However, to construct a theology that gratefully recognizes contributions to Christianity from other faiths while maintaining belief in the universal relevance of the Christ is not only possible but is to be recommended. My aim here is more modest: to suggest how the other religions raise important theological questions for Christians and how one Christian tries to answer them, without attempting to indicate the specific elements these religions contribute to Christian theology.

Professional theologians who read this volume will readily discern that I am not a systematic theologian. I am a missiologist and a missionary practitioner who, along with courses in missiology, has taught history of religions for several years but cannot claim to be a specialist in that field. Whether my professional identity is an advantage or disadvantage my readers will judge.

Therefore, this is not a book for specialists, except that I believe that my suggestions concerning categories and methodology will be of interest to specialists in theology and the history of religions as well as to missiologists. For more sophisticated and comprehensive coverage, experts in these fields will be better served to consult works by such scholars as Gavin D'Costa, Paul Knitter, W. C. Smith, Clark Pinnock and others, and especially the new and massive volume by Jacques Dupuis.

Rather, this book is introductory in nature. It is my hope that it will have a much wider readership than would a volume designed for specialists. If it is read and taken seriously by students in colleges and seminaries and those who teach them, and by ministers and lay leaders in the churches, I shall be satisfied. In short, as I said at the outset, if this book is read by those who desire a rationale for supporting Christian missions among other religions while maintaining both the integrity of their own faith and respect for these other religions and the cultures they have produced, then I will feel that its purpose has been achieved.

E. Luther Copeland
Raleigh, North Carolina
June, 1998

PART I

Introduction, Terminology, and Representative Viewpoints

CHAPTER 1

The New Encounter and the Christian Theology of Religions

THE NEW AWARENESS OF THE RELIGIONS AND ITS CHALLENGE TO THEOLOGY

The New Meeting

ONE OF THE GREAT facts dominating the religious scene today and offering an immeasurable challenge to Christian theology is the new meeting of the religions, largely a post-World War II phenomenon, which has only recently begun to seep into the consciousness of lay Christians. I shall not presume to say how the religions other than Christianity are reacting to the present encounter. I can speak with more confidence concerning my own faith, how it is reacting and especially how I personally react.

From the Christian standpoint, it is difficult to exaggerate the significance of the present meeting with the world religions. I agree with those scholars who say that this new phenomenon is a challenge to Christian theology comparable to the great intellectual crises of the past: the encounter of the early church with the religious variety of the Greco-Roman world, including Greek philosophy; the perceived necessity for the medieval synthesis to cope with the new knowledge seeping into Europe, particularly Aristotelianism; and the challenge of Darwinism in the modern history of the West.[1] The late Anglican missiologist,

Max Warren, an astute student and observer of the times, in 1958 made the prophetic remark that the challenge of the religions to Christian theology would render the issue of science a mere child's play.[2]

What is meant by the new encounter, of course, is not so much that the world has suddenly produced great religious variety, though it is true that there has been a burgeoning growth of new religions in the last few decades. Rather, what is meant by this new meeting of religions is that peoples of the world, especially Western Christians, have come to a dramatic new awareness of religions other than their own, particularly the major religions, and their challenge to faith and theology.

The New Awareness

What accounts for this twentieth-century phenomenon? Why this new consciousness of the challenge of the world religions to Christian faith? There are many factors that have helped produce this new situation, such as the development of modern science, the end of political colonialism, and the vast array of information provided by the study of world religions. Primarily, however, the reason for the new challenge of the religions to Christian faith is that the amazing new means of communication and transportation that characterize the modern world have brought people of other cultures to our very doorsteps, and usually these migrants have carried their religions with them. Conversely, many of us, by virtue of our work, vacation, academic exchange programs, or for some other reason, travel and live abroad for varying lengths of time among people whose faith differs from ours. In one way or another, therefore, we have encountered the major religions in quite a new fashion. It is one thing to think of other religions as something far removed from us. It is quite another matter when they are represented by our acquaintances.

Likewise, Christians of Asia and Africa are forming their own ideas about the religions that are dominant in their areas and that are important components of their own religious and cultural heritage. All in all, therefore, as never before, there is a real encounter between Christianity and other religions as distinct from a more abstract, misinformed, or academic acquaintance.

The Effect upon Theology

This new meeting of the religions has drastically affected the construction of Christian theology. Not too long ago a Christian theologian might teach and write for a whole career and give little attention to the question of Christianity's relation to the other religions. Take the case of the late Paul Tillich, one of the most notable theologians of the twentieth century. It was only late in his career that Tillich began to take the major religions of the world with seriousness and to develop some extensive knowledge about them. By now no theologian worth his or her salt can fail to give attention to this profound issue, and some view it as the most important inquiry that absorbs their thinking, research, and writing. No major branch of Christianity is exempt, although some have been more active and have developed their concern earlier than others.

Also, it is not surprising that a voluminous literature is being produced which grapples with this issue, and that a new theological discipline is emerging, known as *theology of religion* or *theology of religions*.

In addition, it is important to note that the development of the discipline of comparative religions, or the study of world religions, which has increasing prominence, has provided a very impressive array of knowledge concerning the world religions which a Christian theology of religions cannot afford to ignore. It is not my purpose here to recount the facts that the academic study of religions has offered, though I have taught the subject many years and have produced a small book on the subject.[3] Suffice it to say here that any attempt at a Christian theology of religions must be erected upon the foundation of the vast body of knowledge supplied by the study of world religions.

Nor, I suppose, is it to be wondered at that the burgeoning growth of a Christian theology of religions and the huge body of literature which it is producing raises and seeks to answer a very broad range of theological questions, touching upon practically the whole gamut of Christian theology. In later chapters, I shall try to articulate these questions and give at least some tentative and personal answers. Indeed, the identification of these questions and a set of brief answers constitute the heart of this book.

SOME SUGGESTIONS ABOUT CATEGORIES

Now, however, I shall give some attention to the question of categories that the developing theology of religions is employing and how these might be amended. How may different viewpoints be classified?

The Familiar Three

For some time now, the various stances on the question of a theology of religions have been identified broadly as three: *exclusivism, inclusivism,* and *pluralism*. Presumably, these categories are determined primarily by soteriology and secondarily by revelation. Essentially, therefore, *exclusivism* sees little or no good or truth in the religions and claims that nobody, or almost nobody, can be saved without hearing the Christian gospel. Accordingly, those who do not hear and respond favorably to the gospel are excluded from its salvific benefits.

Inclusivism, on the other hand, takes a more affirmative view of the religions, but, like exclusivism, it also believes that no one is saved except by God's provision for salvation in Jesus Christ. However, there is a significant difference: inclusivists believe that many are saved who never hear the gospel and therefore know nothing of the historical incarnation, but that such persons are saved only through the universal redeeming work of God in Christ.

As for *pluralism,* usually pluralists are careful to distinguish pluralism from plurality (a somewhat confusing distinction, since the term *pluralism* is often used simply to denote diversity or plurality of religions). That is, religious plurality means merely that there is a variety of religions, while religious pluralism, as usually understood, is the view that God as Ultimate Reality, Mystery, or some other absolute category, transcends all this variety. Therefore, Jesus is but one bearer of salvation among many; his redemption is valid for Christians, but God has provided salvation for others in various ways.

The Inadequacy of the Familiar Categories

While this threefold categorization is very convenient, I find it also quite inadequate and even misleading. Some who use this terminology and believe it valid—Alan Race, for example, who presumably introduced it—nevertheless criticize this terminology as over-simplifying and "apt to miss the special and particular nuances of any one position."[4]

I have often thought that the frequent positioning of Hendrik Kraemer, the great Dutch historian of religions and missiologist, in the exclusivist camp points up the inadequacy of the terminology. Kraemer's volume, *The Christian Message in a Non-Christian World,* dominated the missiological scene for three or four decades after its publication in 1938. Along with Karl Barth and Emil Brunner, Kraemer is considered to be a dialectical theologian. Although he often expressed quite negative views about the religions, Kraemer insisted, and I think rightly so, that his view both of the religions and their adherents was dialectical.

That is, Kraemer viewed the religions as at the same time responding affirmatively to God and fleeing from God, reflecting the profound ambiguity of human nature.[5] Within the religions one could find the loftiest of ideals and practices but also the most degraded examples of human belief and behavior. He even included Christianity with the other religions under this judgment, claiming that the only advantage Christianity possesses is its unique relation to Jesus Christ. Though Kraemer was very reticent about locating places where the right response to God actually occurred, he claimed that the revelation of God in Jesus Christ was simultaneously exclusive and inclusive, thus apparently applying the dialectic not only to revelation itself but also to the question of who was saved and who was not.[6]

It is clear, therefore, that Kraemer was far too complex a thinker to be put neatly in a box as an *exclusivist*. Indeed, most theologians of religions are not easily classified. They refuse to be bound by our categories.

The inadequacy of the threefold classification is even more apparent when it is realized that the late Lesslie Newbigin is sometimes referred to as *exclusivist*. To my knowledge, Newbigin has never made the familiar claim of exclusionists that persons who are not Christians have no hope of salvation. On the contrary, he has stated specifically that the church is not "the exclusive possessor of salvation."[7] It is not that Christ is absent or inactive where the gospel is not known, but that it is presumptuous to say who are saved and who are not. Newbigin has even said that his view partakes of all three of the familiar positions: exclusivism, inclusivism and pluralism. "It is exclusivist in that it affirms the unique truth of the revelation in Jesus Christ, but *it is not exclusivist in the sense of denying the salvation of the non-Christian. . . .*" It is inclusive in that it does not limit the saving grace of God to the Christian church. It is pluralist because it acknowledges God's gracious presence and work in all human beings.[8] Obviously, then, the application of this terminology to Newbigin is both unfair and inaccurate.

The terminology of exclusivism, inclusivism and pluralism is itself too exclusive! Too many theologians of religion cannot be contained within these boundaries, and some may be all three in various aspects of their thought. It may be better to discuss the thought of theologians individually, without categorizing them. Of course, some of them identify themselves specifically, whether correctly or not, as one or the other of these classifications. Especially do some seem eager to be known as pluralists, and others non-pluralists.

Toward New Categories

If we must have categories—and probably they are necessary—they should be more broadly defined, and it should be recognized that not all of them are mutually exclusive. With tentativeness, therefore, I suggest the following, taking care not to associate them with any particular scholars:

Negativism is the viewpoint that sees nothing, or almost nothing, good or affirmative in the other religions, and no possibility of salvation for their adherents, except maybe for some rare exceptions.

Dialecticism views both religions and their believers at the same time negatively and affirmatively, as exhibiting both good and evil, truth and falsity, nobility and debasement.

Confessionalism recognizes that faith must be nondogmatic. Persons holding this position give witness to their commitment to Jesus Christ and to the meaning of that commitment, but not with a claim for scientific certainty, and not with a derogation of the other religions. There is a certain tentativeness to this position: it maintains an open mind with regard to other religious claims, which it seeks to hear and understand, recognizing, at least initially, that some other religious claim may be more compelling than one's own.

Christocentric Pluralism identifies Christ with the Absolute (also referred to by terms such as the Ultimate or the Mystery). Therefore this view recognizes that the diverse expressions of the Absolute in the various religions are also manifestations of the cosmic Christ. However, the incarnation of the universal Christ or Logos (the Absolute) in Jesus of Nazareth is but one of these manifestations and has validity only for Christians.

Theocentric Pluralism differs from the previous position in that the Absolute is not identified with the Christ. Christian claims have validity for the Christian but not for those who profess some other religious faith. The Absolute transcends the variety of ways in which it is expressed and understood. The incarnation of the Absolute in the Christ, Jesus of Nazareth, is but one of these several revelations.

Regnocentric (or *Soteriocentric*) *Pluralism* insists that the kingdom of God, which I prefer to call *God's new order*, understood as the salvation of human beings from social ills and the manifestation of justice and love in the world, transcends the different religions. All religions may contribute to this realization of the new order, but none can claim superiority or finality vis-à-vis the others.

Paradoxical Pluralism is the view that the Christian is committed to the ultimacy of Jesus Christ as though it were absolute, knowing at the same time that this belief is relativized by other religious claims which contradict it and by an Infinite Mystery which transcends it and all other symbolical expressions of the Ultimate. So there is a *relative absoluteness*.

Non-relativistic Pluralism may be called pluralism only in the sense that it recognizes positive values in the phenomena of religious pluralism. That is, God reveals Godself in the various religions and therefore interaction between the religions is necessary to an adequate understanding of truth. Nevertheless, Christ is neither relativized nor absolutized but understood in the Biblical sense as universal Lord and Savior.

Pre-eschatological Agnosticism is the recognition that a final disclosure of the truth about religious claims must wait until the eschaton. The ultimate revelation of what is true will not be known until the end of history. In some form or other, this view may be true of most of the positions indicated above.

THE PROMISE OF THIRD WORLD THEOLOGIANS

Although the above categories, including those I have suggested, have arisen in the context of Western Christianity, Third World[9] Christians increasingly are contributing to the development of a theology of religions. This may be as good a place as any to discuss briefly these Third World theologians.

The Prominence of Third World Churches

In my judgment, the significance of the rise to prominence of the Christian churches of the Third World as yet escapes most of us Christians. For the most part, these churches are products of the Christian missionary movement stemming from the West. The churches and Christians of this vast area—Latin America, Africa, Asia, and the Pacific Islands—have become more numerous than those of the Western world. That is, the center of world Christian population has shifted from the West to the Third World.

Insofar as I have read the theologians of the Third World, I find their suggestions on the whole promising, among other things, for the future of relations of Christians to persons of other religions, since many of them, notably those of Africa and Asia, live in environments shaped by faiths other than Christianity.

Some of these Third World theologians, especially some from Asia, have adopted the usual type of pluralism, believing that no religion, including Christianity, can claim an ultimate or universally valid revelation. It is very difficult for this viewpoint to escape the charge of relativism, since, in my judgment, it relativizes all claims to revelation. Its acceptance by theologians of Africa and Asia seems a bit surprising, *insofar as they understand the religions as attached to their environing cultures.* Such a viewpoint seems to call into question the validity of the Christian identity of these thinkers. That is, if each religion is inseparably linked to one culture, why did these Third World Christians turn from the religion, or religions, of their own culture to accept a *Western* religion?

The Relevance of Liberation Theologies

Liberation theology is predominantly, though by no means exclusively, a phenomenon of the Third World and an expression of Christian theology, whether the liberation involves residents of Latin America, where it has received its name and achieved most prominence, or Native Americans, African Americans, Africans, Asians, women, homosexuals, or others who seek liberation from some alleged oppression. Usually, these theologies are concerned with the social and political problems of their environment and have a minimal interest in questions of religious pluralism. Certainly exceptions are to be found. For example, some feminist theologians believe that just as male normativeness has led to the oppression of women, so, when one religion is taken as the norm, the result is oppression of the other religions.[10] Perhaps Jon Sobrino, a well-known liberation theologian, is implying something similar when he insists that the theme of the suffering of humanity has priority over themes of cultural and religious diversity.[11]

Latin American liberation theology strikes a responsive chord in parts of Africa and Asia. But Christian theologians of Africa, by and large, are concentrating upon ridding themselves of a servile dependence upon Western theology and recovering the meaning of their own religious heritage, which the missionaries, with some exceptions, had encouraged them to reject. Hence they are engaged in relating Christian faith to the pervasive "African world view."[12]

Unlike Latin American liberation theologies, those of Asia, such as the Minjung theology in Korea or the "Asian liberation theology" of Aloysius Pieris in Sri Lanka, tend to seek vital relations to their particular Asian religious heritages as well as to the dynamic modernization process, which is well-nigh universal in Asia. Even so, Asians who seek to construct a Christian theology of religions, though not absent, tend to be rare—though not as rare as Latin American theologians of religions.

Contributions from Third World Theologians

From the perspective of their missionary significance, the theologians of Africa and Asia seem to fall within one of two categories. On the one hand, there are those whose writings are almost entirely in Western languages, and whose message seems beamed toward Westerners and especially Western Christians. They perform an invaluable service in challenging the Western categories of understanding Christian faith, which tend to be too deeply conformed to Western cultures. Their ministry, therefore, is in large measure a missionary or ecumenical ministry to the West, and a very significant one. On the other hand, there are those whose writings are mostly addressed to their own culture and especially to Christians of their own environment, often in an indigenous language. Thus, in the efforts of these Christians, a missionary ministry to people of their own culture predominates. In my judgment, both of these types of African and Asian theologians who seek to relate Christian theology to their cultures are extremely significant. In fact, I believe they are essential to a truly universal Christianity.

I look for further exciting contributions to a universal Christology by new understandings of the Christ in the particular cultures of the Third World, paralleling the translation of the meaning of Christ by the Logos concept in the Greek context. I expect that, increasingly, the Christ will be meaningfully interpreted by the *Dao* in the Chinese heritage[13] (*Dao* translates *Logos* in the Gospel of John in Chinese: "In the beginning was the *Dao*, and the *Dao* . . . became flesh. . . ."), or the *Dhamma* in the Buddhist[14] (*Dhamma* [*Dharma*] translates

Logos in the Gospel of John in the Burmese Bible, in one of the translations in Sri Lanka,[15] and possibly in other translations in the Buddhist context). Some Christologies have already employed the category of *Ishvara* or some other figure in the Hindu tradition.[16] Increasingly, also, Christ is being understood as the Great Ancestor or as a similar indigenous figure in the African heritage.[17] Not to be overlooked, also, are the very important theological expressions of women of the Third World.[18]

There is great expectation that the process of seeing Christ "through Chinese eyes, Japanese eyes, Asian eyes, African eyes, Latin American eyes," a process already well underway, will help break the bondage of Western Christianity to Greek and Latin constructs.[19]

Nevertheless, most of these Christian theologies of Africa and Asia, although important in their own right, and although seeking to relate the gospel to their own religious heritages, are not attempts at a theology of religions, and that is what this book is about. A few do make such an attempt, and they deserve and receive some representation in this book. For whatever reason, possibly because of facility in English, South Asian Christianity—that of India and Sri Lanka—seems to supply a disproportionate number of these Third World theologians of religion.

ENCOURAGEMENTS TOWARD RELIGIOUS RELATIVISM/PLURALISM

As to Christian theologies of religions, whether a naive lay theology or the more sophisticated preserve of professional theologians, it is obvious that religious pluralism is on the increase. I reiterate that I am not talking about the plurality (diversity) of religions, the significance of which has become much more apparent in recent times. Rather, I refer to the relativistic position of pluralism that I have indicated above, namely, that there is a Transcendent above all religions that relativizes any claims to finality that an individual religion may make. Therefore, all religions partake of revelation but none can claim finality or ultimacy for that revelation vis-à-vis the others. From this perspective, a pluralism that is not relativistic is exceptional.

The vastly increased personal contacts with the religions have encouraged this relativistic type of religious pluralism. Perhaps it was inevitable that a personal knowledge of the sincere adherents of other faiths would raise questions about the normativity and finality of Jesus Christ as Christians have traditionally understood him. Or, more likely and more naively, questions are provoked about the superiority of Christianity. How can I claim that I have a superior religion when I observe the virtuous lives of persons committed to other faiths?

But there are other reasons for the increased popularity of the relativistic type of religious pluralism. In part, the following discussion of these historical factors reflects my conviction that Christian religious pluralism of the variety indicated reflects the development of religious relativism. Of course, there are many kinds of relativism. I reiterate that what I am discussing is religious relativism, which denies the finality of any religious ultimate except that Ultimate which looms behind all that profess to be final, whether the claim be for revelation in Christ, in the Qur'an, in Buddha, and so on.

The Enlightenment

First of all, there is the influence of the Enlightenment. The intellectual movement bearing this name emerged in the seventeenth century, though its roots are earlier, reaching back at least as far as the Renaissance, and it became more pervasive in the century following its beginning, that is, in the eighteenth century. The Enlightenment exalted human reason as the final arbiter of truth. This movement was one of the factors that caused world religions, or what used to be called "comparative religion," to become a discipline for study. But it also contributed to a relativistic attitude toward the religions which, in turn, has been prominent in the development of a Christian theology of religious pluralism.

Religiously, the Enlightenment was accompanied by deism, the view that generally opposed "revealed religion" and insisted upon the primacy of human reason over divine revelation. The deists were monotheists, but they did not accept doctrines of divine providence or miracles. They believed that God had created the universe and then left it to operate on its own, much as a clock maker—to use a hackneyed illustration—would do with a clock that he had made. Many of them naively supported "natural" or "primitive" religion as based upon reason or upon some alleged original revelation that accompanied creation and then ceased. It is not difficult to see how this exaltation of human reason would tend to equalize or relativize world religions when the latter became more adequately understood, and thus contribute to the development of a relativistic variety of pluralism.

There are those who see the "urgent need for human unity,"[20] which is so prominent in the development of a pluralistic theology of religions, as a child of the Enlightenment. It was at the time of the Enlightenment that Westerners began to think in terms of the whole world. Pluralists respond, however, that although this concern for unity certainly stems from the historical background provided by the Enlightenment, religious pluralism cannot simply be attributed to this historical context. A much broader set of factors is invoked.[21]

Modern Science

Secondly, the development of modern science helped to encourage a new "scientific" way of studying the religions and also to encourage a relativistic attitude, which, in turn, tended toward religious pluralism among Christians. This scientific development was undergirded by the Enlightenment, but its beginning is usually dated about two hundred years later, in the nineteenth century. Modern science is very skeptical of unproved absolutes—though of course it does not abandon all absolutes, the concept of an orderly universe, for example, without which science would be impossible.

From the Christian standpoint, science was considered to be especially dangerous because it was understood to oppose or set aside what were usually thought of as the teachings of the Bible. Since the significance of myth (story) as a means of communicating truth had not yet been recognized, religious claims were generally taken quite literally. How could the Bible be true when science had uncovered evidence that the universe was far more ancient than the few millennia indicated by the creation stories in the book of Genesis and the genealogies that followed? How could the account of a special creation of human beings be believed when science taught not only that the story of human development was much older than the Bible seemed to claim but that evolution traced the development of the human species, not from an original special creation of God, but from lower forms of life? Those who believe in the literal nature of the Bible and its inerrancy still have trouble with science.

The result of the combination of these two phenomena of Western history, the Enlightenment and the scientific movement, was a relativizing of religious claims and a shying away from absolutes, which aided in the development of pluralism.

The Study of World Religions

A third inducement toward the acceptance of a relativistic/pluralistic position in religion was the study of world religions itself. As I have indicated, this discipline of study was in some measure a child of the intellectual developments of the West just identified. Since the study of religions claimed to be a science, with the aim of objectivity, it tended to encourage the relativistic position. Indeed, many scholars of world religions, in their laudable efforts toward objectivity, were religious relativists. If scholars perceived both the attractiveness and the failures of all the religions, their negative as well as their positive aspects, it was very difficult to claim final truth for any one of them, particularly in a world dominated by science.

Factors Internal to Christianity

There are indications, also, that there were factors within Christianity itself that encouraged relativism and thus created a climate in which a relativistic pluralism could rather naturally emerge. On the one hand, there was a reaction against science which helped to develop a narrow, intolerant attitude that characterized much of Christian theology. Clark Pinnock has suggested that the restrictive theology of traditional Christianity drove people into relativism.[22]

No doubt Pinnock is right, particularly when one considers the intolerance and arrogance of much of Christianity as we customarily know it even today, whether Catholic or Protestant. The doctrine of *extra ecclesiam nullas salus* ("no salvation outside the Church") for centuries characterized Roman Catholicism. Though Vatican II tended to erode this doctrine, probably it is still believed by many Catholics. This doctrine was paralleled in Protestantism by the widespread conviction, still strongly held by many conservative Christians, that nobody could be saved without receiving knowledge of the Christian gospel from the testimony of some Christian, or from the New Testament itself, which of course involves the testimony of Christians. This kind of negativism almost certainly would tend to drive sensitive Christians in the direction of relativism.

Conversely, Langdon Gilkey sees a source of religious relativism in a combination of factors within Christianity that are associated with the development of a liberal theology: the emergence of an ecumenical spirit, which called into question any absolute claims of one denomination as against another; an inclusiveness with regard to race and sex; a more fraternal relation with the Jews; and a reversal of the dominance of faith over love. These alterations of theological conviction were affected, to be sure, by other factors as well, such as the Enlightenment and the shattering of political colonialism.[23]

Western Colonialism

The mention of colonialism introduces a fifth aspect of the modern world that helps explain the prevalence of religious relativism: sensitivity toward the comparatively long period of Western colonialism, which has come to an end fairly recently. The collapse of the great colonial empires has happened with remarkable rapidity since World War II. Only a few vestiges of political colonialism remain—though, of course, other kinds of colonialism continue, such as economic and cultural imperialism. With the disintegration of political colonialism, a well-established system obtaining for about five centuries was all but obliterated. From the perspective of world history, this is a phenomenon of extraordinary significance.

The memory of political colonialism left many Westerners with a strong sense of guilt for the injustice and cruelty of much of the colonial past. It is commonplace for Westerners to view themselves as perpetrators of the sins of colonialism and for Third World peoples to see themselves as its victims. In most cases both are right.

In it all, Christianity is seen as oppressive, and the Christian mission is viewed as the religious arm of the Western colonial system. If the Enlightenment and the emergence of modern science helped to encourage religious relativism, the post-colonial age has added great impetus to this development, especially among Christians, and particularly Western Christians. The widespread religious relativism of today's world is first and foremost a post-colonial phenomenon. Many contemporary Christian theologians who are relativistic pluralists mention in their writings the influence of the colonial past.

It is not only understandable but appropriate for Western Christians to feel guilty for the history of Western colonialism, the injustice, cruelty, and racist arrogance of which cannot be denied. That the Christian mission, in the light of colonialism, must be radically reformed to manifest genuine humility cannot be overemphasized, as I shall discuss more fully later. Whether it should lead to religious relativism and thus to a relativistic Christian pluralism is quite another question.

The Revival of Culture in Asia and Africa

In the sixth place, the cultural renascence in Asia and Africa that has attended the end of colonialism has contributed to the increase of religious relativism in general. Hence, it probably is one of the factors that has helped produce religious pluralism among Christians. As a significant aspect of this cultural revival, the religions of these great continents have likewise experienced spiritual renewal, contradicting a Western view prevalent early in this century that the religions of Asia and Africa, being unable to withstand the secularization of the modern world coupled with the effects of Christian missions, were on their way to an early demise. In many instances, these religions have come to a new sense of maturity, ready to address their own cultures, and indeed the rest of the world, with assurance that they have a relevant message for all people. They feel that they have withstood the onslaughts of the West, especially the challenge of Christian missions. This victory, they claim, has been achieved in the disadvantageous situation of colonialism and Western dominance. So the religions are now ready to face Christianity without a sense of inferiority.

I remember well, for example, the many Hindus in India whom I met in the 1960s who expressed the belief that Hinduism had a message that the West badly needed. One old Hindu gentleman raised a question about the high incidence of mental and psychological disorders in the West and indicated that the Hindu concept of karma, the law of cause and effect, was in large part the answer to this problem. Indian people, said he, accepted their lot in life with equanimity because they believed it to be the working of their karma, what they had done in a previous existence.

In the new era, when we Westerners already feel guilty about colonialism and are imbued with ideals of tolerance, it is relatively easy to believe that the Christian claim for the universal relevancy of Jesus Christ should be set aside. To be sure, the motivation to be scrupulously fair and to seek the best in assessing other religions is thoroughly in accord with Christian ethics, with the Golden Rule, for example. However, surely this moral imperative does not justify Christians in minimizing or setting aside Christian faith convictions because these might be viewed as an attitude of cultural or religious superiority.

The Attraction of Hinduism

In the seventh place, honesty compels me to say that one of the factors that has helped increase religious pluralism among Christians is the absorptive allurement of Hinduism. It was to be expected that when Christians got to know Hinduism, they would be attracted to it, especially in a relativistic age. The apprehension that all religions are essentially one, although to be found widely dispersed in human culture, is certainly characteristic of Indian thought. Raimundo Panikkar equated the pluralistic attitude to which he himself was committed with a "plunge into the Ganges,"[24] the holiest river of Hinduism. Obviously, he meant an immersion in that religion.

Hinduism is considered an ethnic faith and is largely confined to India and Indians who have emigrated to other countries. Though such Indian immigrant communities are relatively small, Hinduism is the faith of close to 800 million people in India itself. And India is second only to China as the most populous country in the world. Not only in terms of its impressive spiritual content, therefore, but also in terms of its numbers of adherents, Hinduism is quite significant. No doubt its importance is even larger than its membership.

Actually, Hinduism is a kind of overall name given to the great diversity of religions that have grown in the fertile soil of India through its long history. In addition to its great antiquity and spirituality, Hinduism greatly prizes its almost incredible diversity and its belief that none of its varieties can claim final validity. Though it may seem contradictory, the Hindu view is that a religion, such as Hinduism, that recognizes the relative validity of all religions, is superior to one that does not. This combination of antiquity, diversity, and relativism exerts a strong pull upon the hearts and intellects of contemporary Westerners with their sense of guilt for Western colonialism. Therefore, it is perhaps inevitable that the attractiveness of Hinduism would encourage the development of a relativistic Christian pluralism.

The Appeal of a Relativistic Pluralism

All of which means, finally, that on the face of it, the position of relativistic pluralism is quite attractive, particularly in the contemporary period. As I have already indicated, it is quite difficult to sustain a religious claim to some kind of revelational ultimacy in our present environment. It is very appealing just to admit that all religions are similarly, if not equally, valid.

The relativistic viewpoint relieves the Christian of the burden of a religious mission based upon belief in the universal Lordship and Saviorhood of Christ.

As I have indicated, I believe that Christians who subscribe to the usual pluralistic theology of religions have great difficulty avoiding religious relativism. Although most insist upon the continuance of the Christian mission, if they can no longer make the claim for the ultimate and universal significance of Jesus Christ, what they are proposing is inevitably a greatly altered Christian mission. I reiterate that some insist upon using the terminology of pluralism while resisting the temptation to relativize.

Of course, the right question is not whether a relativistic religious pluralism undercuts the Christian mission. This is essentially a pragmatic question. Of more ultimate concern is whether this kind of pluralistic position can be squared with truth, insofar as we can know truth. That is, is it consonant with the Christian claim for a definitive revelation of God in Jesus Christ? Of course, a Christian pluralistic theology of religions that relativizes Christian faith cannot be sustained together with an acceptance of the traditional doctrines of Trinity and Christology. I believe that these doctrines, arising as they did in the context of Jewish monotheism, are grounded in the cross of Jesus Christ followed by the resurrection. If so, then the very basis for Christian faith argues for a high Christology and a doctrine of the Trinity.

Of course, I am not insisting upon the necessity of the formulation of these doctrines in the categories of Greek philosophy as they were expressed in the early Christian Councils. At least since the late Karl Barth, who emerged into theological prominence early in the twentieth century, there has been the tendency to go beyond the Greek formulations with their fundamental concept of God's impassivity and to construct Trinitarian and Christological doctrine on the basis of Biblical concepts.[25] More recently, there have been deliberate attempts to understand the world religions according to Trinitarian concepts.[26]

I myself feel keenly the attractiveness of the position of a relativistic Christian pluralism. I suppose that the appeal has always been there but it is considerably enhanced in our time. However, I believe that this type of pluralism calls for a radical reassessment of the Christian understanding of incarnation, atonement, and revelation, and I doubt that Christian faith can sustain such without serious detriment to its truth claims.

However, it is time to introduce, even if briefly, some representative theologies of religions.

CHAPTER 2

Theology of Religions: Representative Viewpoints

PLURALISM ITSELF, THEREFORE, has become a significant and controversial issue in the developing Christian theology of religions.[1] Among several Christian theologians known for their espousal of pluralism are John Hick, Paul Knitter, Aloysius Pieris, Raimundo (Raymond) Panikkar, and Stanley J. Samartha. A brief treatment of the view of each is included below. I have also included a notice of the non-relativistic pluralism of Jacques Dupuis, though his perspective is that of a kind of mediating or borderline pluralism.

PLURALISTIC VIEWPOINTS

John Hick

John Hick is a prominent philosophical theologian and an English Presbyterian.[2] Hick has called for a "Copernican revolution" in the Christian theology of religions. Just as the old earth-centered, Ptolemaic conception of the universe had to be abandoned when the solar-centered Copernican view appeared, so our Christianity-centered orientation must be given up. We must realize that the center of the universe of faiths is God and not Christianity or any other religion.[3] (Though Christians have acted as though Christianity were the center, probably most would say, if asked, that Christ is the center of the universe.) Elsewhere, Hick has referred to this revolution in Christian thought as a "paradigm shift."[4] Realizing that the positing of God as the center of the world of faiths would exclude religions such as Theravada Buddhism which believe in no personal deity, Hick later began to add the terms "the Divine," "the Transcendent," "the Ultimate," "the Real" to "God," with a preference for "the Real."[5]

All the major religions are the results of "seminal moments of religious experience" that occurred during the Axial Period (which coincides roughly with the millennium before Christ). Each of the great world religions thus emerged in relative isolation from the others, and their revelatory experiences were differently conditioned by their diverse cultural and historical circumstances.[6]

As for the claim for the uniqueness and normativity of Jesus Christ, Hick indicated that what Christians call the Incarnation is mythological language to express the experienced fact that we have really found God and the salvation of God in Christ. Therefore, Hick can recognize a similar validity to the claims of others to have found God and salvation differently. Thus, wrote Hick, "we can say that there is salvation in Christ without having to say that there is no other salvation than in Christ."[7]

In the book he co-edited with Paul Knitter, Hick developed ideas based on the move from an absolutist to a non-absolutist view of Christianity, after the pattern of Ernst Troeltsch.[8] Thus it is clear that Hick gives up traditional Christology, including the idea of the death of Jesus as cosmic event with universal consequences, in favor of what he calls a "pluralistic" view.

In a recent book, Hick has set forth his pluralistic position in the very interesting format of a dialogue with fictitious characters: a philosopher, Phil, and a theologian, Grace. In this volume, as in his earlier writings, he has articulated his view with considerable sophistication, lucidity, and attractiveness.[9]

Paul Knitter

Paul Knitter is an American Roman Catholic theologian who has published quite widely in the field of a theology of religions.

In his early writings, Knitter identified himself as one of those theologians who are in transition from "ecclesiocentrism" to "christocentrism" and now to "theocentrism." According to Knitter, these theologians see the world religions, including Christianity, as a "unitive pluralism" in which each has a "complementary uniqueness." Their uniqueness, therefore, is a unique relatedness and interdependence. For Knitter, "no longer the Church (as necessary for salvation), nor Christ (as normative for salvation) but God as the divine mystery is the centre of salvation history and the starting point for religious dialogue." God has really spoken in Jesus and all must hear this message. But God has spoken in others also and they too must be heard.[10]

However, at that time Knitter himself expressed some doubt about his newly adopted viewpoint: "Is Christian tradition being preserved or maimed in this new model?" he asked. Then he seemed to answer his question by a presumed insight from liberation theology that "orthodox discernments about uniqueness and finality . . . are perhaps not all that important as long as we, with all peoples and religions, are seeking first the Kingdom and its justice" (Matthew 6:33).[11]

In a later essay in a book of which he was a co-editor, Knitter followed up this suggestion by seeking to show how certain insights and guidelines from liberation theology can move us toward a "pluralistic theology of religions." To put it altogether too briefly, Knitter proposed that liberation theology, in starting the interreligious dialogue from the perspective of God's preferential option for the poor, may direct us to a soteriocentric rather than either a theocentric or a Christocentric position. Thus it may help us to avoid the "slippery slopes of relativism" and to retain a Christology that transcends both exclusivism and inclusivism in a new pluralism that preserves the content and power of authentic Christian witness.[12] Knitter has tried to take seriously criticisms leveled against him by such theologians as John Cobb, Avery Dulles, and Hans Küng, that he had forsaken Christology for theology.[13]

In still more recent writings, Knitter has filled out much more comprehensively what he means by a soteriocentric or a kingdomcentric pluralism.[14] Not only has he set forth a new kind of pluralism, he has also articulated a new Christology and a new understanding of mission. It is to be doubted, however, whether his suggestion of a pluralism that takes as its starting point salvation rather than Christology as such, will be any more satisfactory than his theocentric pluralism. Though Knitter would rather avoid the term "pluralism" and be known as a correlational theologian of religions, he admits that he is still "a pluralist—though a chastened one."[15]

Knitter almost completely ignores the sufferings or death of Christ as relating to the salvation that he provides. Rather, he sees salvation as expressing the love of God through the love of neighbor, or as following God's call to transform this world from one of division and injustice into one of love and mutuality. While this interpretation certainly emphasizes the teaching of Jesus, in my judgment it represents a truncated Christology that can hardly escape "the slippery slopes of relativism."

Aloysius Pieris

Aloysius Pieris, a Roman Catholic monk of Sri Lanka, was educated not only in the West but earned the first doctorate ever awarded a non-Buddhist by the University of Sri Lanka. He understands profoundly the theology and practice of both Buddhism and Christianity, and he has written with discernment about the relation of these two faiths.[16] Yet he is conversant with the other religious systems of Asia as well. It is significant that the Vatican has recently denounced him for his theological views.

Pieris has also manifested a strong concern with liberation theology, and he has written insightfully about how Asian liberation theology differs from its Western counterparts. In An Asian Theology of Liberation, published in English in 1988 (and two years earlier in German), he was saying that the only door that could admit Jesus to Asia was "the soteriological nucleus or the liberative core" of the Asian religions, and he devoted several pages to an attempt to show that these religions did indeed have such a liberative nucleus.[17]

In this same book, Pieris included a chapter the primary subject of which was what he termed "a third world theology of religions." In this discussion, he indicated the relevance of the primal religions, and he pointed out, with illustrations, the revolutionary urge in the various religions of Asia. He concluded that the starting point and object of interreligious cooperation was not theology, or God-talk, but liberation (on this point his thinking is similar to that of Knitter); that technology, the result of an evolution of human beings from the biosphere to the noösphere, is distorted and dehumanized by acquisitiveness; and that the enculturation of Christianity in Asia depended upon its being framed within a Third World understanding of the gospel—the gospel understood not as reactionary but as revolutionary.[18]

That is, Christianity must accept both the spiritual riches of Asia and the blight of Asia's poverty. Although poverty is degrading when it is imposed on others by the extravagant life style of some, it is ennobling when accepted voluntarily as a revolutionary protest against its imposition.[19] Thus, Pieris insisted that the fulfillment of the Biblical mandate in Asia depended upon Christians appropriating "the religiousness of the poor" as their own spirituality.[20]

In a lecture delivered in 1978, Pieris was already claiming that the call to what he termed the kingdom of Christ and the call to the church were to be distinguished. The latter was reserved for a relative few (the "little flock"). Accordingly, the appropriate relation of the Christian to "good, practicing Buddhists" and adherents of other religions was to understand how the "kingdom preached by Christ had already germinated in them" and therefore to encourage them to be better Buddhists or better believers of whatever religion they professed—except in the cases of that minority who were called to identify with the Church—in order to support further development of the kingdom in them.[21] His viewpoint still seemed to be Christological and inclusivist.

Later, in an essay included in the volume edited by Hick and Knitter, Pieris, as would be expected from a contributor to that book, identified with a pluralistic viewpoint, though there is some indication that his espousal of pluralism was related to a disappointment not only with exclusivism but also with inclusivism (was any other view available to him?). He noted that both exclusivist and inclusivist views led to an impasse. By this route, the Buddhist ended up claiming the superiority of Buddha just as the Christian insisted upon the superiority of Christ.

The issue, as Pieris understood it, is not the claim for uniqueness. Hardly any Buddhist would dispute the uniqueness of Jesus; nor would Christians dispute the uniqueness of Gautama. Everybody is unique.[22] Rather, the problem is in the claims that Buddhists and Christians make for the absoluteness of their respective savior figures. Both see either the Buddha or the Christ as an absolute medium of salvation. The only way the absoluteness of Jesus as medium of redemption can be maintained is a Christology that sees Jesus on the Cross in a double ascesis in which Jesus himself became utterly poor and at the same time struggled for the poor.[23] But Pieris asserted that even this claim will be an empty boast until the followers of Jesus demonstrate in their own lives this double ascesis, voluntarily becoming poor and also struggling on behalf of the poor.

Sad to say, Pieris may be asking for an impossibility. Will more than a small minority of Christians ever accept voluntary poverty and identification with the poor in their struggle? Pieris may well be right in his suggestion that it is only at the eschaton that the true path of salvation "will be recognized by name."[24] So it appears that Pieris retained something of a traditional Christology, even in his confessed pluralism. Even so, he did not view his Christology as competing with Buddhology but as complementing it as both religions worked together for the liberation of the poor of Asia.[25]

Raymond Panikkar

Raimundo (Raymond) Panikkar is a Roman Catholic theologian, born in Spain of a Roman Catholic mother and a Hindu father. He has entered deeply into the world of Hinduism and his theology is often identified with an Asian viewpoint. His statement is frequently quoted that the "good and bona fide Hindu is saved by Christ and not Hinduism, but it is through the sacraments of Hinduism . . . that Christ saves the Hindu normally."[26] Here Panikkar is voicing a familiar concept among Roman Catholic theologians, namely, that adherents of the religions other than Christianity are saved through the "sacraments" of those religions, though this salvation is usually thought of as provisional. Also, as the quotation and the title of the book quoted (*The Unknown Christ of Hinduism*) suggest, his approach is Christological, and it is the Logos Christology that he characteristically employs.

Nevertheless, Panikkar's thought is complex. By the Logos incarnate in Jesus Christ he means the eternal Logos who "can appear, differently but really, in other traditions and historical figures besides Jesus."[27] The "cosmotheandric principle," or the eternal Christ, has many historical names of which Jesus is one.[28] Even in the article that placed Panikkar within the pluralistic camp he set forth a very inclusive Christology.[29]

It is remarkable and puzzling that Panikkar, in the essay in which he identified with pluralism, while clearly basing his discussion upon his view of the Trinity, yet never mentioned the book that so provocatively articulated his Trinitarian concept.[30] This strange omission is in spite of the fact that Panikkar listed seven of his publications against the background of which he wanted his essay to be understood.[31] He made it clear that "the mystery of the Trinity is the ultimate foundation for pluralism."[32] Yet this "mystery that is at the beginning and will be at the end" Panikkar identifies with the Christ.[33] So Panikkar remained Christological even in his pluralism.

Some have thought it strange that Panikkar allowed himself to be identified with the viewpoint of pluralism at all, though he certainly did so in the volume edited by Hick and Knitter.[34] Rowan Williams stated that "Panikkar is clearly an uncomfortable ally for the more familiar 'pluralist' case."[35] Panikkar continued to speak of the "christic event" as having a certain crosscultural relevance and of "Christianness" as denoting the effects of Christianity in the other religions.[36] He even joined with Cobb in what Paul Knitter interpreted as a sharp criticism of the quest of Knitter, Hick, Wilfred Cantwell Smith, and others for a "common source" of the world religions.[37]

Nevertheless, the question of whether Panikkar is actually a pluralist seems to be answered if one realizes that Panikkar's

Logos Christology itself is different from those Christologies that carefully evaluate expressions of the cosmic Logos by the standard of the Logos made flesh in Jesus of Nazareth. If the Christ itself is a universal "principle" capable of being incarnate in many cultures or religions without any one of these manifestations being determinative, then in effect there is little difference from the theocentric pluralism that posits a transcendent "God" or "Reality" as the standard under which all religions are relativized. Panikkar's pluralism, is not a theocentric but a Christocentric pluralism.

Stanley J. Samartha

Stanley J. Samartha, a distinguished ecumenist and theologian from India and a member of the Church of South India, like Panikkar, is quite alert to the environment of Hinduism. He was included in the volume, *The Myth of Christian Uniqueness*, edited by Hick and Knitter, as a representative of pluralism. Though a theocentric pluralist, Samartha called for a theocentrism which includes Christocentrism.[38]

Though previously Samartha seems to have been an inclusivist,[39] in the volume edited by Hick and Knitter, he rejected "both exclusiveness and its patronizing cousin inclusiveness" in favor of what he called the "relational distinctiveness of Christ" and a "theocentric christology."[40]

Still more recently, in a substantial volume, Samartha offered a comprehensive view of what he believed Christology must be in a pluralistic world.[41] There are many statements in the book that elaborate upon the claim for the necessity of a "theocentric Christology." For example, Samartha says that "Christology is larger than soteriology, and theology larger than christology. . . . God alone is the source of all salvation."[42] He notes that "Paul, in spite of his radical Christocentrism, is extremely careful to retain the ultimacy of God." And he quotes Oscar Cullmann as saying that "the total faith, as reflected in the New Testament, is theistic, that is to say monotheistic, and secondarily christological."[43] He is quite critical of the doctrine of the Trinity, not only because its Greek categories of thought are alien to Indian thinking, but also because it makes it all too easy for Christians to move from the affirmation that Jesus is the Christ to the claim that he is God.[44] For Samartha, this claim for the oneness of Jesus with God, that is, the Trinitarian claim, or a Christology from above, compromises the basis of all monotheistic faiths.[45]

In a thoughtful discussion of Christian missions, Samartha declared that Christians must openly proclaim the Lordship and Saviorhood of Jesus Christ. However, it is difficult to see how Christians could affirm Jesus as Lord and Savior, at least if they mean to say that he is Lord and Savior *universally*, without a high Christology and the doctrine of the Trinity, which were designed, as I understand it, not to set aside but to preserve both a high Christology and monotheism. Cannot the revelation of the meaning of God and also the retention of the mystery of God, the necessity of both of which Samartha rightly insisted upon,[46] be accomplished by the kind of Christological and Trinitarian faith to which informed Christians ordinarily seek to witness? It is difficult to escape the judgment that Samartha's Christology is not only revisionist but reductionist and that he falls in the radical theocentric pluralism camp of Hick and others.

Jacques Dupuis

Jacques Dupuis is a Roman Catholic, a Belgian Jesuit, who has had considerable experience both in India and in Rome. In 1997 Dupuis published a massive volume that may be considered his *magnum opus*.[47] In fact, it is not an exaggeration, in my opinion, to call the book "a truly magisterial accomplishment," as does one of the scholars cited in a book jacket blurb.

In what constitutes over half the pages of the discussion of this large book, the author transports us through an "Introduction" and a "Part One," consisting of several chapters, to set the context of his constructive discussion. He carries the story of the Roman Catholic Church through the Biblical material relating to the religions, the cosmic Christ in the early Fathers, the narrow stance of "outside the Church, no salvation," what he calls "substitutes for the Gospel," that is, such strategems as a chance after death—which I would prefer to call "extraordinary applications of the gospel"—to the theological perspectives surrounding Vatican II and the postconciliar magisterium on religion, which has complemented and gone beyond Vatican II's limits. He closes Part One with a chapter on the contemporary debate over theology of religions.

In this large introductory section of the book, Dupuis is at the same time comprehensive and concise, fair and charitable, and unfailingly insightful. I believe that his main points are two: First, it is no longer adequate for a Christian theology of religion simply to view religious pluralism as a matter of course and an empirical fact. Rather, it is necessary to seek the root causes for pluralism and to ask what role the religions play in the redemptive plan of God for the universe. Concerning this issue, Dupuis believed that Vatican II was inadequate and needed to be filled in by the postconciliar magisterium of the Church.[48] He inquired about the prospect for a mutual convergence of the religions with cross fertilization but with the preserving of their differences.[49] Secondly, a new theological method must be invoked, called by some *hermeneutical theology* and by others *global theological method*. In any case, it must be a method that takes seriously the text, or the given of faith, the historical context, and the interpreter. In a word, it must be both deductive and inductive.[50]

In his crucial chapter, "Jesus Christ—One and Universal," he insists upon a Christological Trinitarianism and steadfastly refuses all reductionisms. Yet he chooses language very carefully, opting for the terms *constitutive* and *relational* to communicate the meaning of his Christology. By *constitutive*, he means that for Christian faith, the death-resurrection of Christ has universal significance, sealing between the Godhead and the human race a bond that can never be broken. By *relational*, he means to indicate the relation between the path that is in Jesus Christ and the various paths of salvation seen in the other religions.[51] Yet Dupuis refuses to use the language of absoluteness either with regard to Jesus or Christianity. "The reason is that absoluteness is an attribute of the Ultimate Reality of Infinite Being which must not be predicated of any finite reality, even the human existence of the Son-of-God-made-man." Though Jesus Christ is universal Savior, only God is the absolute Savior.[52]

The Christology with which Dupuis works is the Logos Christology of John's Gospel. He sees both the Noachic covenant and the revealing, redemptive work of the Johannine Logos as universal, not only before the incarnation but up until now as well. Yet this is a Trinitarian Christology. It includes not only the work of the Christ but also "the unnamed action of the Spirit." Like Ireneaus, Dupuis understands the Word (Logos) and Spirit as the "two hands" of God.[53]

Dupuis assigns a positive value to religious pluralism. This pluralism is not only *de facto* but also *de jure*, not only a matter of fact but also a matter of principle. For example, he writes approvingly of Pieris's interpretation of the "gnostic agape" of Buddhists and the "agapeic gnosis" of Christians.[54] In the *saccidananda* (being-consciousness-bliss) of Hinduism he recognizes elements of truth and grace that can complement the Christian understanding of truth.[55] He sees both a "relational unity" and a "historical and eschatological convergence" of the religions.[56]

In a word, what Dupuis envisions is not fulfillment in which Christianity completes the fragmentary truths found elsewhere. Rather, it is a "mutual complementarity," by which Christianity and the other religions may mutually enrich and even transform each other. So he speaks of "complementary values and convergent paths."[57]

Yet I suggest that Dupuis, though writing a "Christian theology of religious pluralism," can never satisfy what he calls the "protagonists of the pluralistic model," such as John Hick, Paul F. Knitter, and Stanley J. Samartha,[58] not only because, negatively, he renounces their relativistic or "revisionist" Christology, but also because, positively, he retains too much of the Biblical and historical tradition of the Christian church. Actually, Dupuis claims a certain priority (one might even say, superiority) for Christianity vis-à-vis the other religions. For example, he cites approvingly J. S. O'Leary's claim that the other religious traditions represent "particular realizations of a universal process which has become preeminently concrete in Jesus Christ." So, throughout history, the religions converge with the mystery of Jesus Christ but not by equal paths.[59]

Thus Dupuis' viewpoint, though set forth in more detail, does not differ significantly from the perspective of his fellow

Roman Catholic, Gavin D'Costa, or from that of Anglican Kenneth Cragg, both of whom are included below under "non-pluralistic viewpoints." If he is a pluralist at all, Dupuis can only be called a "non-relativistic pluralist," which to me means a mediating or borderline pluralist. Of course, the whole matter is one of terminology. The problem is that the old threefold classification of *exclusivism, inclusivism,* and *pluralism* defined pluralism as a kind of religious relativism. Obviously, Dupuis does not fit this kind of category.

NON-PLURALISTIC VIEWPOINTS

Most Christian theologians reject the pluralistic understanding of religions as traditionally understood. These non-pluralists constitute a considerable variety. They include Roman Catholics, Orthodox, Anglican and many varieties of Protestants. They range all the way from conservative to liberal theologians. For purposes of space only a few can be included here.

Gavin D'Costa

A theologian worthy of notice is Gavin D'Costa, who, like Aloysius Pieris, is both Roman Catholic and South Asian, in his case Indian. D'Costa has written two notable books, one of them critically analyzing the pluralistic theology of religions of John Hick and the other setting forth D'Costa's own view, which he identified as *inclusivism*, between exclusivism and pluralism.[60] In addition, D'Costa edited the important volume, *Christian Uniqueness Reconsidered: The Myth of a Pluralistic Theology of Religions*, published in 1990, to which he contributed the preface and an essay. Obviously, the book was a response to the volume edited by Hick and Knitter and published three years earlier, entitled *The Myth of Christian Uniqueness: Toward a Pluralistic Theology of Religions*. Both of these collections of essays were published by Orbis.

D'Costa claimed that an inclusivism that paid careful attention to Trinitarian doctrine could reconcile the particularity dear to the exclusivists and the universality emphasized by the pluralists. Christology set within Trinitarianism guarded "against an *exclusive identification* of God and Jesus as well as against a *non-identification* of God and Jesus." Therefore, it legitimated the claim that "Christ is *normative*," but not "exclusive or absolute in revealing God."[61]

The Holy Spirit leads us into a deeper knowledge of God in Christ, as Jesus had promised, in part by what the Holy Spirit is doing within the other religions. Viewed in this manner, the other religions are necessary to the completeness of Christianity.[62]

In addition, the inner relations of the Trinity give us a model for understanding what is our mode of being, which is loving communion, love of neighbor co-essential with love of God, and crucified, self-giving love as normative. It is in this Trinitarian understanding that liberation is grounded. Accordingly, D'Costa deemed quite unsatisfactory Knitter's idea that the absolute that all must serve is not God or Christ but the kingdom[63] and its justice, because Christians do not know what love and justice are except by our relation to God, Christ, and the Holy Spirit.[64]

The Spirit also gives us "narrative space" in which we can listen to the testimonies of persons of other religious faiths, with the result that our own false conceptions of Christianity may be laid bare and corrected. In the process of sharing our narratives and listening to the narratives of others, not only will our own inadequate and false interpretations of our faith be set straight, but also Christianity will be indigenized, as we adopt elements from other religions and cultures according to their own narrative structures. In it all, that which the Spirit reveals to us will glorify Christ and the Father.[65]

Georges Khodr

An example of an Orthodox theologian who does not espouse pluralism is Georges Khodr, Greek Orthodox Metropolitan of Mount Lebanon at Beirut, a diocese of the Greek Orthodox Patriarchate of Antioch. In an article first published in 1971, Khodr stated his belief that the Holy Spirit must guide us in tracing the presence of Christ in the spiritual life of representatives of the other religions. He also called attention to the

Logos tradition in the Church from Justin Martyr onward,[66] a tradition that Khodr rightly claimed has been taken seriously by Orthodox theologians.

Khodr was looking forward to the eschatological unity of all who belong to Christ, "both those whom the Church will have baptized and those whom the Church's bridegroom will have baptized" (quoting Nicholas Cabazilas). I take it that by the former category he means those who have been called into the membership of the Church in its earthly pilgrimage, and by the latter those who, outside the visible Church, have nevertheless belonged to Christ. Khodr also indicated that it is not so much a question of adding people to the Church as it is identifying the "Christic values" in the other religions and showing their adherents Christ as the one who unites and fulfills them in his love. They will come into the Church naturally, said Khodr, "when they begin to feel at home in it as the Father's house."[67]

In a later article,[68] Khodr further elaborated upon some of the themes of the earlier statement. Particularly, he is careful to show the relevancy of the Trinity to the matter of Christianity's relation to the other religions. He believes that ordinary lay persons are apt to have a "monohypostatic" concept of God[69] that overemphasizes the historical Jesus and the incarnation of God in him. On the contrary, wrote Khodr, the "hypostatic independence" of the Trinity must be maintained. Accordingly, the work of the Holy Spirit in revelation of God in the other religions must be appreciated. After all, Pentecost is not a continuation of the incarnation of God in Christ but its consequence. The church is based upon the twofold work of Christ and the Holy Spirit, two economies that are both reciprocal and independent.[70]

Yet it is Christ—the eternal Logos who is larger than the historical Jesus—who is hidden everywhere within the religions, and it is "the Christ who is received as light when grace visits a Brahman, a Buddhist or a Muslim reading their Scriptures or performing their prayers." Nowhere does God promise that all humanity will be converted to Christianity. Rather, God is as fully interested in persons of other religious traditions as in us Christians. Such a person is "as unique as a

Christian, equally loved by God, possibly a source of edification for fellow human beings and a place of Epiphany."[71]

Therefore, our approach to the other religions must be one of radical humility and vulnerability. Its result is not a syncretism that confuses the Christian message with other messages or a destruction of the genuineness of the other religions by hastily incorporating them into Christianity. "A very severe and continuous critique needs to be undertaken in order to recognize what is Christlike"[72] in the religious sphere outside Christianity, and indeed in spheres that are thought of as non-religious, for Christ is present in poetry and art as well. In this article, also, Khodr affirmed eschatology, in which God's salvation will be experienced as much broader than the Christian circle. The approach he is advocating, wrote Khodr, is neither that of exclusiveness or inclusiveness, but of affinity or similitude among religions, since Christ is the "typos par excellence of every being and dispensation."[73]

Kenneth Cragg

Kenneth Cragg, an Anglican missiologist, in a large volume entitled *Christ and the Faiths*, provided a statement of his mature thinking on the question of interreligious relationships.[74] Cragg wrote with insight, honesty and sensitivity, not only concerning Islam, his specialty, but also Judaism, Hinduism, and Buddhism. In a method he called "cross-reference" theology, he attempted to show how these great religious systems might be affected by their encounter with Christianity both to their own enrichment and to that of Christianity. By cross-reference theology, Cragg meant a theology of mission in retrospect, which takes into account historical experiences both of the Christian and the other, and is open to the hospitality to be found in other faiths and to the necessity of its own hospitality in relating to them.

Yet Cragg posits no easy relationship. For example, he disagreed with John Cobb's statement that "Christians can retain but transcend personal selfhood in a way that corresponds with the Buddhist dissolution of the self." Cragg asserted that the locus and the theme of selfhood in these two faiths cannot be equated. For the Christian, selfhood is received, however it may be interpreted or reinterpreted, while for the Buddhist, the self must be given up as illusion.[75]

Cragg deplored what he believed to be the premature closing of the Canon of Christian Scripture, restricting its concepts of cultural encounter to the Mediterranean world, the world of Palestine, Greece, and Rome. Thus the Scriptural writers themselves had no chance to relate to the diverse world of Asia. Since there seems to be no possibility of reopening the Canon, its cultural inadequacy must be filled in by a cross-reference theology, both to correct and expand the insights of the Church's liturgy and theology and to relate positively to the great religions.

Any Christian concept of the pre-incarnate Logos must seek out and treasure evidences of the work of this Logos in the sacred writings and cultures of the various peoples. The Church must continue its mission, then, with appreciation of the diversity within which it must operate. Whenever it finds within the religions elements of truth, it must gladly recognize these as evidences of truth already "Christian" before the Christian gospel arrived. The Church in the new situation remains the custodian of "the Gospel of the blessed God," to which it continues to give its loyal witness.[76]

Norman Anderson

A much more conservative statement is that of Norman Anderson, Anglican evangelical, specialist in Islamic law and missionary to Egypt. Anderson indicated that he firmly believed that some of the unevangelized will be saved, just as Jews were saved before Christ in the situation of an imperfect revelation. This salvation is by means of the redeeming work of God in Jesus and his cross, an atoning event which is applicable to all times and places. Wherever salvation occurs, it is by means of grace apprehended by faith, that is, by throwing oneself upon the mercy of God. Anderson fully expected that there would be those who, though never hearing the gospel while here on earth, would find on the other side of the grave the one God who had saved them without their understanding it at the time.[77]

As to the theological meaning of the religions, Anderson could not accept without qualification any of the common views that see the religions as products of an original revelation to be fulfilled in Christ, as systems deriving not from God but from the devil, or as constructs originating from human attempts to solve life's mysteries. Rather, he sees the religions as resembling a "patchwork quilt." They exhibit elements of truth that must be of divine origin, elements that are definitely false and of demonic origin, and also much that represents human aspirations for the truth.[78]

Anderson also raised the question whether there is any "saving structure" in the religions other than Christianity. Here he was referring, of course, to the views of some contemporary Roman Catholic scholars, who were saying that adherents of other religions may be saved by the "sacraments" of these faiths. Anderson indicated that he could not go nearly that far. Yet he recognized that there are components of all religions through which God can speak, and that converts from other religions often believe firmly that God was in contact with them in their pre-Christian experience.[79]

John B. Cobb, Jr.

John B. Cobb Jr. is a prominent American Methodist theologian and son of missionaries to Japan. Though a liberal thinker, Cobb holds firmly to Christology in his approach to other religions. He has even written that "to sacrifice belief in the incarnation for the sake of dialogue would not only impoverish [Christians] but would also take from us our most potential gift to the dialogue partner." It is through deepening this crucial conviction of incarnation that "Christian faith moves toward its own transformation through openness to all faiths." And this "process of creative transformation," which leads to a universality in theology, is to be identified with Christ himself.[80]

Cobb envisioned the possibility that Christianity and Buddhism, the religion other than Christianity to which he has given the most study and thought, might be enriched by their mutual internalization. A possible result would be that both the transformed existence of the Buddhist and the individual personal existence of the Christian would merge in some postpersonal form of existence in a fuller expression of universal community. Such an eschatological community not only of persons but of all things would be the perfection of the incarnation already attained in Jesus Christ.[81]

In a more recent essay,[82] Cobb insisted that he remained "Christocentric" as opposed to those, like Knitter and Hick, who had moved away from Christocentrism to what they termed a theocentric position. He rejected their view as positing a common essence of all religions and not really allowing the diverse religious traditions to be unique within themselves. In other words, a view that had already decided beforehand that each religion was a product of the revealing work of God was not really open.

Cobb claimed that faith in Jesus Christ is future oriented. That is, to believe in Jesus is to share his hope of the coming realm of God. Cobb stated

> . . . that a tradition in which Jesus Christ is the center has in principle no need for exclusive boundaries, that it can be open to transformation by what it learns from others, that it can move forward to become a community of faith that is informed by the whole of human history, that its theology can become truly global.
>
> . . . The Christianity that emerges will be . . . one more step toward the fullness that is represented by the coming Realm of God.[83]

With such openness to other religions, Christianity has the possibility of becoming a truly global faith. Since Cobb believed in this radical openness of Christianity, he could claim that his view moved beyond the usual categories, even "beyond pluralism," as his essay's title suggested.

Lesslie Newbigin

Notable among more conservative Protestant theologians is the late Lesslie Newbigin of Great Britain, missionary to India, ecumenical statesman, and highly respected missiological and theological thinker. Newbigin has always held tenaciously to the "finality of Christ," as the title of one of his many books indicates.[84] In a more recent book, he again articulated his bedrock principle: "the Christian mission rests upon a total and unconditional commitment to Jesus Christ as the one in whom all authority inheres."[85] Newbigin's Christology, as the first point in his six affirmations indicated below will indicate, is that of the cosmic or universal Logos. Yet he also emphasized the necessity of Trinitarian doctrine. He had pointed out earlier that the work of mission is participation in the mission of the triune God.[86]

In his definitive statement of missionary theology, Newbigin gave a succinct critique of John Hick's call for a Copernican revolution in theology in which he strongly opposed Hick's point of view.[87] Then he discussed and found wanting several Christian estimates of other faiths, ranging all the way from the claim that the other religions and ideologies are totally false to the notion that they are media of God's salvation.[88] Newbigin articulated his own view of how the Christian understands the religions by six affirmations,[89] which I can give here in little more than outline.

1. All of the created world, including every human being, is already related to Jesus Christ as the eternal Word in whom God is present in the fullness of the divine being. Thus the presence and work of Jesus are universal in human religion and beyond it, and Christians will meet other men and women who do not acknowledge Jesus as Lord, "not as strangers but as those who live by the same life-giving Word."

2. The other side to this bright picture is our human tendency to pervert God's good gifts of grace into instruments of our pride and self-will, thus cutting ourselves off from God and the abundant life God intends for us. The revelation in Jesus teaches us that God purposes the salvation of all persons, but it does not entitle us to assume that this salvific intention can be accomplished by ignoring or bypassing the historic event by which it was in fact revealed and effected, that is, the cross of Christ.

3. The accomplishment of God's saving purpose is by means of a real history at the center of which are the definitive events concerning Jesus of Nazareth and the end of which is the actual consummation of all history and not simply that of individual human lives abstracted from the life of society and the world.

4. Therefore, "an essential part of the history of salvation is the history of bringing into obedience to Christ" the rich diversity of ethical, spiritual and cultural treasures which are God's gift to humankind. In the history of Christian missions, wrote Newbigin, we can see at least the beginnings of the fulfillment of this "plan for the fullness of time, to unite all things in him, things in heaven and things on earth" (Ephesians 1:10).

5. Thus, the church, in its pilgrimage through history, faces the world neither as the sole possessor of salvation nor as the fullness of what others have only in part, but as sign, first fruit or witness of that redemption that God purposes for all the universe. It relates to the world dialogically, bearing its witness to the world and at the same time discovering in other places beyond itself the riches of God that belong to Christ and that deepen and broaden the church's understanding.

6. Finally, Newbigin suggested a model for this dialogical relationship in the form of a diagram by Walter Freytag, a German missiologist, depicting a cross at the foot of several staircases, each of which represents the ethical and religious achievement of the various cultures.[90] Actually, however, this ascent of staircases has taken human beings farther away from the place where God meets us, that is, the cross. Therefore, the representatives of all religions, Christians included, must descend the stairway in a *kenosis*, a self-emptying, to meet at the foot of the cross. We must see ourselves not as possessors of God's truth and holiness but as witnesses to them, standing under their judgment.[91]

After the volume edited by Hick and Knitter appeared, Newbigin once more addressed problems of religious pluralism. Whereas previously his criticisms of this position had centered upon John Hick, he now discussed the various writers of this newly published volume and found their pluralistic viewpoints wanting.[92] He added to his earlier discussion, which I have outlined briefly above, a critique of the oft-asked question: "What happens to the non-Christian after death?" He claimed that this was the wrong question, because it is a question that God alone can answer, because it abstracts individuals from their actual position in the ongoing history of the world, and especially because it starts with the question of the ultimate happiness of the individual and not with the question of God's purpose and glory. He reiterated his conviction that the goal of missions is the glory of God, and once more he stated his belief that persons who are not Christians may well be among the saved.[93]

Ajith Fernando

Some of the recent literature produced by those generally associated with "conservative evangelicals" tends to be somewhat irenic and appreciative of other religions. A Christian thinker who represents such a position is the Sri Lankan, Ajith Fernando, National Director of Youth for Christ in his country. Fernando's book is entitled *The Christian's Attitude Toward World Religions*. Like other fundamentalists, Fernando believes in the infallibility and inerrancy of the Christian Scriptures, but he states his case with considerable moderation.

Fernando claimed that as an effect of general revelation the religions have in them certain elements of truth that the Christian may use in presenting the gospel, as Paul did in his message to the Athenians (Acts 17: 16-34).[94] Much of Fernando's book is an exegesis of Paul's Athens speech, and I thoroughly agree with him that Paul used sound missionary principles in addressing the Gentile audience at Athens. After all, Paul's missionary effort at Athens was not a failure. Because of his witness, several of the Athenians became believers, including two who are specifically named (Acts 17:34). I suggest that any who denounce Paul's missionary approach in Athens as a failure should go to

Banaras (Varanasi), India, address the Christian message to the Hindu pundits there and see how many become Christians!

Fernando demonstrated additional generosity in calling for scrupulous fairness in comparing Christianity with the other religions and in acknowledging that Christians can even learn from these other faiths.[95] However, for him, all the religious systems other than Christianity are "untrue at their heart,"[96] and they are in no way vehicles of salvation.[97] Accordingly, the only hope for salvation for those outside the Christian circle is for them to hear the good news of what God's grace has provided in Christ and accept this offer of grace in faith.

Two chapters of Fernando's book are devoted to the attempt to establish the fairness of God in light of the impossibility of salvation for any without personal knowledge of Christ.[98] The principal arguments are that all persons are under the sway of sin and that there are differing degrees of punishment, with those who have never heard the gospel but have been sincere seekers coming off with less severe penalties than those who have sinned willfully. Fernando recognized that some "unanswered questions about God's fairness" may remain in the minds of some. For them, he recommends that they accept with humility what God has taught in God's inerrant Word, the Bible, and that they leave judgment to God.[99]

Clark H. Pinnock

Much more positive on this subject than Fernando is Clark H. Pinnock, a Canadian Baptist theologian, whose pilgrimage has carried him from a strict fundamentalism to a progressive evangelicalism. The title of his major work in this field, *A Wideness in God's Mercy*, indicates that it is no narrow exposition, as indeed it is not. Pinnock hoped that his book would "change evangelical thinking on this subject" and help to set a new agenda for evangelical theology.[100]

Pinnock rejected the "fewness" doctrine, that those who are saved will be few, and for this purpose he carefully reviewed the Biblical evidence. Accordingly, he affirmed the doctrine of general or cosmic revelation by which people with no knowledge of Jesus Christ nevertheless receive a knowledge of

God.[101] While rejecting the concepts that understand the Incarnation as myth and the Trinity as a basis for a theocentric pluralism, Pinnock affirmed a cosmic Christology in the context of trinitarianism. The eternal Logos incarnate in Jesus of Nazareth is not confined to a time or a place. The triune God of which the eternal Logos is the second person, is a missionary God. Pinnock was at pains to establish this contention by a survey of the Bible.[102]

As to the religions themselves, Pinnock concluded that the Bible understands religion on a broad spectrum, ranging all the way "from truth to error, from nobility to vileness."[103] As to what the religions would be in the future, nobody could predict, since they were dynamically changing and God could do with them in history whatever God chose. Meanwhile, Christians should give their witness faithfully, in the confidence that all the religious impulses of human beings would be fulfilled in Christ in a kingdom in which none of the historical religions would appear, including Christianity, a kingdom with only God and the community of the redeemed. This means that Christians are to be liberated from bondage to triumphalism, since they hope not for the victory of the churches but only for the victory of Christ. They are freed both for the kind of evangelism that seeks followers of Christ rather than members of Christian churches, and for truth-seeking dialogue that may transform Christianity as well as the other religions.[104]

Though Pinnock rejected universalism, it was only after he had given it a sympathetic treatment. And he came out clearly for a this-worldly salvation and an encounter with Christ in the world beyond death by which many who had not heard about him in this life would have opportunity for eschatological redemption.

Pinnock realized that this claim for a broad access to God would call into question the motive for Christian missions. But he insisted that the true motive is not saving people from wrath or hellfire but proclaiming the good news of the kingdom, "not an announcement of terror, but news of God's boundless generosity." The purpose of Christian mission involves not only proclamation and church planting but also a strategy for transforming the world and history.[105]

The title of Pinnock's book, chosen from words of Frederick Faber's great hymn, "There's a Wideness in God's Mercy," indicates the generosity of his intention. He resisted the pluralism of theologians such as Hick and Knitter. He even pulled back from the teaching of Roman Catholic theologians such as Rahner that the religions other than Christianity could be vehicles of salvation. Nevertheless, he certainly is to the left of most "evangelical" theologians, and his theology is quite a contrast to strict fundamentalism.

In the remaining chapters I shall attempt to present my own view, which, though set forth much more briefly than most, may have the virtue of being broader in scope.

PART 2

Theology of Religions and Theological Questions

CHAPTER 3

Articulating the Questions

The Scope of the Questions

As I HAVE remarked previously, it is not surprising that the voluminous body of literature on a theology of religions is addressing a broad range of questions, covering nearly the whole gamut of Christian theology. Though it is likely that a discussion of these various questions can be found in the literature as a whole, to my knowledge nobody has identified the questions or attempted a well-rounded discussion of them. My purpose is to suggest what these questions are and to discuss them one by one in order to set forth a brief and tentative statement of what I believe the constituents of a theology of religions should be. Perhaps my particular contribution is more in the suggested questions than in my discussion of them, though I trust that the latter, though brief, is not without its value.

Of course, I am not claiming that the list of questions I have suggested below is exhaustive, or that the questions themselves are mutually exclusive. Other scholars may wish to include other issues, organize them differently, or give them fuller treatment. I am only insisting that the questions I have identified represent my way of delineating and organizing them and my conviction that they need to be understood and addressed. Let me emphasize, also, that I am not attempting a comprehensive discussion of the various aspects of Christian theology. I seek only to give a lucid treatment of the various facets of Christian doctrine that are directly affected by the Christian encounter with world religions.

The Questions Themselves

1. The question of the *revelational norm*. By what norm does the Christian make judgments concerning the religions?

2. The question of *clues for understanding*. What is the clue, or what are the clues, for understanding theologically the relation of Christianity to the other religions?

3. The question of the *source*, or *sources*, of the religions. From what sources do the religions originate and grow?

4. The question of the *scope of revelation*. Is there revelation of God outside the circle of the Biblical revelation? If so, where is this revelation to be found?

5. The question of *salvation*. Does revelation outside the Christian orb have salvific significance?

6. The question of the *Christian mission*. Is there a Christian mission? If so, what is its nature?

7. The question of *evangelistic expectations*. Should Christians expect members of other religions to confess that "Jesus Christ is Lord"? If so, how should these Christians relate to their own religious heritage?

8. The question of the *missions of other religions*. Does God have a mission for the other religions? If so, how should Christians understand and relate to it?

9. The question of *interreligious relationships*. From the Christian standpoint, how should the religions relate to each other?

10. The question of a *special relationship to certain other religions*. Does the Christian religion have a special relationship to some other monotheistic faiths? to all monotheistic faiths?

11. The question of the *nature of the church*. What is the church, and what does the nature of the church mean vis-à-vis the other religions?

12. The question of *salvation (sacred) history*. How should Christians understand the relation of salvation history to other histories or to world history?

13. The question of the *temporal future of religions*. What is the Christian vision of the future of religions within history?

14. The question of the *eschatological future of religions*. What kind of eschatological future should the Christian envision for the religions?

And now, with some tentativeness, I suggest my own answers to these questions.

THE CHRISTIAN NORM

By what norm does the Christian make judgments concerning the religions? Is the norm the Biblical revelation as a whole? the revelation of God in Jesus Christ? some general or philosophical understanding of the meaning of religion, such as a common essence?

A Common Essence

The positing of a common essence of religion means that one steps outside the Christian circle and takes a stance from which even the Christian revelation itself may be judged. Therefore the norm can hardly be called a Christian one. Several decades ago, the idea of a common essence was harshly judged and found wanting by Hendrik Kraemer, who saw the religions as unique, all-inclusive systems of life.[1] On this point I think Kraemer was right, though he seems to have failed to recognize the dynamic, changing character of the religions. Of course, he was conservative, or neo-orthodox, like Karl Barth and Emil Brunner. Now, however, there are liberal theologians who insist that no common source or common essence theory can assess the truth claims of a tradition from outside it. Among these are John Cobb, Langdon Gilkey and Raimundo Panikkar.[2]

The Total Biblical Revelation

Nor is the Biblical revelation as a whole a sufficient norm for a theology of religions. While along with most Protestants, I accept the Scriptures as the "sole and sufficient authority for faith and practice," I insist upon certain canons for Biblical interpretation, all of which, I believe, have relevance for the Christian understanding of the religions.

> (1) I accept Martin Luther's concept of Christ as the norm by which the Scriptures are to be understood. If the Scriptures in their entirety comprise the norm, then it is likely that doctrines of inerrancy and infallibility will be invoked, and these doctrines, apart from whether they can be adequately defended—and I believe they cannot—constitute unnecessary baggage to carry into one's attempt to relate to persons of other faiths.
>
> (2) Where teachings of the Bible seem to be in contradiction, I choose the instruction that appears to me to be more in keeping with the qualities of love and fairness that I believe to be central Biblical teachings.
>
> (3) I look for instances of the influence of contemporary culture upon Scriptural teachings, believing that in certain cases apparent scriptural teachings must be set aside as human or cultural traditions rather than the word of God.
>
> (4) I accept teachings and practices from sources other than the Bible, including, of course, the other religions, so long as these teachings and practices are consistent with the spirit of Christ—even if they were not literally taught and practiced by him.
>
> (5) I take seriously the interpretations of Scripture made by the believing community of Christians, both past and present, and in so far as possible I accept them. However,

on some important matters sincere Christians differ and churches have been wrong in the past. In the final analysis, God alone is Lord both of the conscience and the reasoning powers of the individual. Therefore, the individual Christian must make up his or her mind about the authority and interpretation of Scripture and be willing to live or die by these convictions.

If some object that we cannot make ethical judgments concerning the Scriptures, I reply that we make such determinations every day, whether or not we are aware of it. As is often observed, all of us have our own canon of Scripture, and, by the way we live if not by our words, we pick and choose those parts of Scripture that we consider authoritative. Also, within the Bible there is sanction, not only for questioning what God is reputed to have said but of God's own character. Consider, for example, Abraham's ethical query as to God's intended actions. "Shall not the Judge of all the earth do what is just?" he asked (Genesis 18:25).[3] And Abraham was known as "the friend of God" (James 2:23). Surely God must be more ethical than Abraham (or than I) or we are really in trouble! Then there is the example of Jesus. He enunciated doctrine more authoritative than the Mosaic law. Jesus declared, "You have heard that it was said, . . . but I say to you . . ." (Matthew 5:21-48).

The Revelation in Christ

Therefore, my choice for the norm by which the Christian makes religious judgments is the revelation of God in Jesus Christ. My own faith is unabashedly Christ-centered. The norm is the self-revealing of God, the incarnation of God in Jesus Christ. While it is entirely proper, even necessary, for the Christian student or scholar of religion to have some general, inclusive definition by which he or she may understand religious phenomena quite beyond the Christian circle of belief, Christian faith itself can never accept such a definition as theologically adequate. When Christians set about to construct a theology of religions, they must look to the very center of the Christian revelation, which is Jesus Christ.

THEOLOGICAL CLUES

What is the clue, or what are the clues, for understanding theologically the relation of Christianity (or the Christian revelation) to the other religions? general revelation? natural theology? the activity of the cosmic Logos? the universal Holy Spirit? the Trinity?

This question is similar to the first, concerning the norm, but it is by no means identical. The norm is foundational to the theological clues I have suggested above. For example, if one accepts as the norm the revelation of God in Jesus Christ, then the clues suggested above must themselves be subjected to that criterion. Some cannot stand the test.

General Revelation

A case can be made from the New Testament for general revelation, a Christian designation sometimes equated with natural theology, though the two do not mean quite the same. For example, in Acts 14:16-17, the apostles, Barnabas and Paul, declare that God "has not left himself without a witness . . . in giving rains from heaven and fruitful seasons." Also, the Apostle Paul spoke of a revelation of God through the natural world, by which the divine nature has been clearly seen and understood (Romans 1:18-20), and through the human conscience, to which revelation appeal may be made in the judgment (Romans 2:12-16). And in Hebrews 1:1, the (general?) revelation of God through the ancient prophets is contrasted with the revelation "in these last days" through the Son.

The Incarnate Logos

It seems to me, however, that the testimony of the New Testament as a whole is more favorable to the idea of the revelation of God through the Logos who was incarnate in Jesus of Nazareth than to a general revelation. Accordingly, for the theological clue for understanding the relation of Christianity to the other religions, I opt for the universal revealing and redeeming activity of God through the cosmic Logos, or the Son, implemented by the Holy Spirit, as Gavin D'Costa, John V.

Taylor, and others have claimed,[4] and therefore involving the Trinity. It seems to me that this selection of a clue is consistent with the norm of the revelation of God in Jesus Christ. I shall give a bit more discussion of this Logos Christology later. From this viewpoint, revelation is never "general" but "personal." Even the revelation of God through nature is inseparably related to the agent of creation who is also the agent of revelation, namely, the Logos, the second member of the Trinity.

Of course, it is specifically in the Gospel of John that the Son—Word or Logos—is declared to be the revealer of God and at the same time the one through whom all things were created (John 1:1-9, 14-18). However, the language of Colossians 1:15-20, that the Son is "the image of the invisible God," that "in him all the fullness of God was pleased to dwell," and that God is reconciling everything to God through the Son and "the blood of his cross," implies that the Son also is the revealer of God, for it can hardly be conceived that the revealer is separated from the creator and redeemer. The same is true of the language of Hebrews 1:1-4, which describes the Son as "the reflection of God's glory and the exact imprint of God's very being," through whom all things have been created and sins purified. (It is possible that Revelation 3:14 refers to the Son as agent of revelation—calling him "the faithful and true witness"—but it is likely that the reference is to the earthly life of Jesus rather than to the cosmic dimension of his existence.)

Moreover, this recognition of the Son as revealer is not entirely absent from the Synoptic Gospels. Both Matthew and Luke quote Jesus as saying, "All things have been handed over to me by my Father; and no one knows the Son except the Father, and no one knows the Father except the Son and anyone to whom the Son chooses to reveal him" (Matthew 11:27, Luke 10:22; the reference here, also, may be to the revelatory work of the human Jesus and not to the cosmic Logos).

It is especially from the Johannine teaching that the concept of the cosmic dimensions of the Logos as the second member of the Trinity is derived and is posited as the theological clue for understanding the relation of the Christ to every person and of Christianity to the other religions.

The Cosmic Logos—With Certain Understandings

However, some words of caution are appropriate. In the first place, always the cosmic Logos must be understood in relation to the incarnate Logos, that is, to the historical manifestation of God in Jesus of Nazareth. Divorced from the incarnation, the concept of the Logos can too easily come to mean anything the theologian employing it wishes it to mean; especially can Logos be used as a sanction for the position in the theology of religions that I have called "Christocentric pluralism," which involves a relativizing of the revelation in Christ that I cannot accept. The cosmic revelation must be subject to the revelation in the incarnate Logos and not vice versa.

Secondly, where does one look for the traces of this life-giving Logos? It is common to look among the sages. Thus, Justin Martyr named the Greek philosophers Socrates and Heraclitus as belonging among the Christians, since they not only partook of the divine Logos—as did all persons—but also lived according to the Logos.[5] In fairness to Justin, however, it should be recognized that he also indicated "not only philosophers and scholars but also artisans and people entirely uneducated" as knowing in part the eternal Logos.[6] In modern times, a less ambiguous emphasis on the sages may be seen in the late A. C. Bouquet, a prominent exponent of a Logos Christology, and others who have followed his thought. Though Bouquet acknowledged that there was "a gap between the sages and Jesus," it was to the "sages and prophets" who were not Christians that he looked in his effort to identify those who were living in tune with the Logos.[7]

While I would not rule out the quest for the revealing work of the Logos among the sages and prophets, from Jesus' own evaluation of character it seems much more appropriate to seek those who have been enlightened—and redeemed—by him as eternal Logos among the lowly: the poor, the mourners, the meek, those who long for righteousness, the merciful, the pure in heart, the peacemakers, those persecuted for righteousness's sake (Matthew 5:3-10; Luke 6:20-22), and those who serve the needy (Matthew 25:31-46).

Thirdly, I believe it is erroneous to look for the revelation of the Logos only in those concepts or terms that seem to parallel

Logos in meaning or function. In this regard, perhaps *Dao* and *Dharma* are the best examples, though the literal meaning of all three terms is quite different. Indeed, the concept of Logos itself, as understood by the Greeks who originated it (interpreted variously by the Greek philosophers, but essentially as a dynamic principle of Reason by which the whole creation is ordered) has to have Christian content poured into it before it can represent the Son of God. If one looks for the expression of the Logos only in similar terms, then, it could be inferred that the revealing Logos has not been active in certain cultures, at least not to the extent that this activity may be discerned in the Daoist and Buddhist (and Hindu) religions or cultures from which the two terms indicated above derive. In my judgment, such an inference is not warranted.

While taking seriously these words of caution, therefore, I reiterate that I believe the Logos concept gives us the best theological clue for understanding the relation of Christianity to the other religions.

SOURCES OF THE RELIGIONS

From what source or sources do the religions originate and grow? Are they products of demonic deception, of human imagination and creativity, of divine revelation?

I believe I have just identified all three of the most likely candidates for answers to the question: demonic deception, human creativity and divine revelation. And I believe that this judgment may take Christianity as its model, since all three are to be seen within Christianity.

Revelation

Of course, the third of these, divine revelation, as being operative in the origin and development of Christianity, is axiomatic for Christians. But adherents of other religions also believe that their religions are products of some revelation of the Ultimate, though they may characteristically use other terms to describe this process. And who is to say that they are wrong? To admit revelation in other religions is not to set aside the normative and ultimate revelation in Jesus Christ. But revelation itself requires a separate treatment as an answer to other questions I shall consider later.

Demonic Deception

But what about demonic deception? By this term, I do not mean the work of personal beings known as demons. I mean what I believe to be a much more profound concept of evil, a mysterious power of deception and other wickedness existing in the universe that goes beyond the sum total of evil human wills. In addition to the personalizing of evil in terms of demons and Satan, the prince of demons, the Bible, it appears to me, teaches this more sophisticated and deadlier concept of evil as well. I, myself, have been in situations where attempts at good within the Christian community seemed to be thwarted by an inexplicable power of evil far more profound than the defects of the relatively good human beings involved. Evil, then, is profound, subtle and deceptive and is to be taken with utmost seriousness.

I am reticent to speak of demonic deception in the beginning of Christian faith or of any other religion. When a religion is first born, it is likely to be at its purest. However, if what appears to be demonic deception is not present from the beginning, it soon asserts itself. For example, how can one view persecuted Christians becoming the persecutors, conversions at the point of the sword, the Crusades, the Inquisition, the anti-Jewish pogroms, the too-ready Christian sanction of the Nazi terror, racism in general, and the most virulent homophobia as anything less than demonic?

Paul Tillich expressed it aptly:

> Demonization of the holy occurs in all the religions day by day, even in the religion which is based on the self-negation of the finite in the Cross of Christ. The quest for unambiguous life is, therefore, most radically directed against the ambiguity of the holy and the demonic in the religious realm.[8]

Perhaps this is the place for a word about the necessity of recognizing and confronting evil both in one's own religion and in others. Nothing justifies a namby-pamby spirit when it comes to combating evil. Just as denominational commitment should not cause us to ignore denominational evils, and just as an ecumenical spirit should not blind us to what is wrong within Christianity as a whole, so a desire for good interreligious relationships is no excuse for the sanction of wickedness within the larger circle of religions. Unfortunately, it is within religion that the most abhorrent forms of evil too often assert themselves—another indication of the presence of the demonic. It has been noted by Langdon Gilkey that "in our own century intolerable forms of religion and the religious have appeared," and that in each case an absolute religion sanctioned the oppression of a class, race, or nation. All such tyrannies, said Gilkey, must be resisted.[9] And, of course, he was right. Most of us know when something is evil. And we must follow the dictates of an enlightened conscience or of the best ideals that our religion teaches or of both. We must oppose evil, whether it claims to be religious or not.

Human Imagination

As for the other prospective candidate for the origin and development of religions, namely, human imagination and creativity, certainly it is well represented in the origin and growth of Christianity. In the early development of our faith, for instance, there are examples of outstanding personalities such as the Apostle Paul whose remarkable gifts are not solely due to some special endowment of the Holy Spirit. Indeed, sometimes Paul admitted that he had "no command from the Lord" but that he was giving his own opinion as a "trustworthy" servant of Christ (1 Corinthians 7:25, for example). Not only did Paul manifest trustworthiness; he also demonstrated ingenuity and creativity, qualities derived not only from the Holy Spirit but also from his original creation and from his environment and training.

Or take certain aspects of church polity that were patterned after the organization of the Roman empire. Surely these are examples of human creativity. They can hardly claim divine inspiration. Or again, in certain Christian denominations there are rather remarkable systems of finance or Christian education and the like. Are they not due to human ingenuity, and would it not tend toward idolatry to claim that they are divinely inspired?

Therefore, upon the model of Christianity, to the revelation at the center of which I am committed, I am inclined to see all three of these factors, demonic deception, human creativity and divine revelation, as present in religions generally. In this understanding I believe that I am in essential agreement with Lesslie Newbigin,[10] and even more obviously with Norman Anderson, who sees in the religions traces of all three, the divine, the demonic and the human. I think his metaphor of the religions as resembling a "patchwork quilt" is especially appropriate.[11]

All of the above I have written because I believe that the Christian must make some evaluation of the sources of the origin and development of the religions, including first of all his own. It would be preferable for members of each religion itself thus to identify its sources. But it seems impossible for any of us to avoid the responsibility of seeking an understanding of the other religions upon the basis of one's own faith. In the Christian context, it appears to me that this is one important part of what is meant by a Christian theology of religions.

THE NATURE AND SCOPE OF REVELATION

But what about revelation itself? Is there revelation of God outside the circle where the Biblical revelation is known? or is there discontinuity between the biblical revelation and the other religions? or fulfillment? If God is revealed outside the orb of Biblical knowledge, is this revelation to be found in human culture generally, in the religions specifically, or in both?

The first of these questions I have already answered affirmatively. I believe that there certainly is revelation of God outside the Christian circle, through the universal Logos.

Discontinuity

The term "discontinuity" I find entirely inappropriate. Though Hendrik Kraemer had used it sparingly already, he singled it out in a paper prepared for the world conference of the International Missionary Council at Madras, India, in 1938. The paper's title itself, "Continuity or Discontinuity," suggests this emphasis.[12] The point was to juxtapose the position of Karl Barth, which Kraemer approved, with that of Clement of Alexandria, which Kraemer castigated as a "common essence" theory. Several years later, he repeated the term "discontinuity,"[13] somewhat apologetically, it seems to me—or as nearly apologetically as Kraemer could bring himself to be!

I have often wished that Kraemer, from whom I have learned much, had never used the term. He seemed primarily to be concerned with the concepts of a common essence in the religions and of a fulfillment of these religions in Christ, both of which he rejected. So far, so good. I have already expressed my resistance to the idea of a common essence. I also feel that the concept of fulfillment must be treated quite critically. Christ may well fulfill the aspirations of the human heart, but since the religions have their own distinctive quests, which differ from the Christian quest, the concept of fulfillment seems invalid as applied to the religions. On the other hand, if there is revelation of God outside the Biblical revelation, for example, through the Logos—and Kraemer admits that such happens[14]—then surely there must be some continuity of that revelation with the Biblical revelation. Hence my dislike for the term. It seems to confuse rather than enlighten.

Revelation in Culture

But does God reveal truth not only in the religions but in human culture generally? I believe that the answer must be affirmative. In primal societies a distinction is not ordinarily drawn between culture and religion. For example, is there not at least a hint of divine revelation in a remarkable ceremony of the fierce, cannibalistic Asmat people of New Guinea? According to Don Richardson, peace is attained between different Asmat tribes through the enactment of a new birth ritual. Children of each of the warring tribes are passed over the prone backs of the fathers and then between the legs of the mothers of the opposing tribe. Then the children are treated as babies for as long as the ritual lasts.[15] The dramatization of new birth seems obvious. Is this ceremony religious or cultural or both?

Or, to take an example from what would be considered a more sophisticated culture, what about the "passive resistance" concept articulated and employed effectively by Mahatma Gandhi? Though Gandhi validly claimed some religious sources for this concept, it operated primarily in the area of politics and was espoused by some who professed no religion. Therefore, was it essentially cultural or religious? How can one determine? Or what about the American Constitution and its Bill of Rights? That this document and its origins are cultural would be generally recognized. Possibly some would claim the authority of divine revelation for it. Though I would not view our Constitution as a product of revelation, is it completely independent of such revelation?

I believe that if "the love of God is broader than the measure of man's mind," as we often sing,[16] then God's concerns, also, are far wider than our religions. According to the Scriptures, the creator God pronounced every aspect of the created order "very good," and the first creation story contained what many call a "cultural mandate," that is, to "be fruitful and multiply" and to "have dominion" over the whole creation (Genesis 1:28). Since God in creation gave a sanction to culture, it is hardly conceivable that God's revelation would carefully exclude human culture, or, indeed, that some clear-cut distinction can be made between secular culture and religion. Culture may well be the medium through which the values of a given society are expressed, but surely one could not argue from Scripture that God is not concerned with human culture. The history of the Bible is not only a history of salvation but also of a salvation that operates within culture. Indeed, human cultures are to be saved in the eternal city or God, are they not? God has created far more than individuals, and faith is never isolated from culture. Surely culture is one of the areas in which God is revealing the truth of things.

Revelation in Religion

Now, if revelation of God is to be found in culture generally, how much more must this be true in what we usually view as the more restricted field of religion! At the point where the human being is reaching out for God and searching for the deepest meanings of the universe and of life, surely God is revealingly present. Indeed the Scriptures indicate that this is the case. Through the prophet, God spoke an encouraging word to the Israelites in exile: "When you search for me, you will find me; if you seek me with all your heart" (Jeremiah 29:13). Does not this promise express a basic principle, as indeed the New Testament witnesses, namely, that God meets us at the point of our religious quest, that if we approach God, God will come to us also (James 4:8)? If so, this fact does not exclude ways and recipients of such revealing that may be quite surprising, even revelations received by an unwilling recipient, as seems to be the case of Balaam and possibly of his donkey (Numbers 22:7-24:25)![17] (It should not be overlooked, too, that Balaam, not to mention his donkey, was outside the circle of the covenant religion of Israel.) Surely the revelation of God is to be found both in culture and in religion.

I do not mean to say, of course, that revelation is to be found in all religions equally. Rather, I believe that revelation is not absent in the religions other than Christianity. It is hardly reasonable to assume that God has nothing to do with any of the major religions that have been so prominent in developing important cultures and that still retain the allegiance of millions of people and afford them ethical idealism. Christians, then, as I see it, believing in the normative and definitive revelation of God in Christ, do not find the other religions to be completely alien. Christians expect to discover that the God they know in Christ has been present in the religions long before Christians came in contact with them.

SALVATION

But what of salvation? Does this revelation outside the Christian orb have salvific significance? Is there salvation outside the circle where the Christian message is known? Is there possibility of salvation for someone who has never heard the name of Jesus or for someone who has heard but has not accepted? Are the religions themselves possibly vehicles of God's saving grace? Is salvation, wherever and whenever experienced, related to the life, death, and resurrection of Jesus Christ?

Revelation and Salvation

There are many Christians, of course, who believe that whatever knowledge of God there is outside the Biblical revelation is only revelatory and without redemptive intent. That is, for those who never hear the gospel in this life there is no hope. This is clearly the view of Harold Lindsell[18] and of many fundamentalists who share his theological perspective. It is also the view expressed by Don Richardson and by Ajith Fernando in books that, unlike Lindsell's, show some generosity toward the other religions and see in them evidences of general revelation.[19] It seems also to be the concept of at least one Neo-Orthodox theologian, Emil Brunner,[20] who could hardly be considered as conservative as these just mentioned. Still other Christians practically nullify their recognition of the possibility of salvation for those who have never heard the gospel by making them unusual or insignificant exceptions.[21]

To me it is inconceivable that the God we know in Jesus Christ would offer divine revelation to billions of people with no intention thereby to save them. God's purpose is a redemptive purpose. God is portrayed as the Shepherd who goes forth to find a lost sheep and then brings it home rejoicing (Luke 15:3-7), or as the Father who celebrates when his prodigal son returns home (Luke 15:11-32). To God's banquet of salvation "many will come from east and west and eat with Abraham and Isaac and Jacob" (Matthew 8:11; see also Luke 13:29). God does not want any "to perish, but all to come to repentance" (2 Peter 3:9; similarly, 1 Timothy 2:4).

If it is objected that all these New Testament references are to Gentiles who will have heard the Gospel through the Christian mission, then one must ask about the "saints" of the Old Testament who obviously knew nothing of Jesus and his cross. Were they not saved? And, in addition to Israelites, some of the Old Testament characters who were apparently redeemed were Gentiles who presumably had not even received the revelation given to the Hebrews. What about Melchizedek and Job, for example, and all those preceding Abraham, including Noah? The prophet Malachi even states that God's name is great among the Gentiles, "from the rising of the sun to its setting," and that a "pure offering" is presented to God in all these nations peopled by Gentiles (Malachi 1:11). Is it to be assumed that none of these people outside the orb of the Christian revelation who know and worship God sincerely are among the saved?

Who Are the Saved?

As for the question of those who have heard the gospel but have not accepted it, how can we know who has *really* heard the gospel? Maybe some have only heard a message that they did not understand, delivered by a person, the arrogance of whom they thought they understood all too well! Maybe some have rejected the message of Christianity because they knew only a Christianity that contradicted the message. Some, therefore, may have refused the Christian message for Christian reasons. There is danger, therefore, in the common practice of Christians to castigate those who have rejected the "gospel" as evil.

Then it hardly behooves us to hold a "we-and-they" or "us-and-them" concept, does it? We certainly do not know who is saved and who is not. We do not even know whether all of us Christians are saved, do we? Presumably, the line between those who are accepted by God and those who are not is a line that cuts through the Christian community as well as the larger world community. Only God knows who is going to make it in the judgment and who is not. Is it not an unseemly conceit to assume that we know?

If it is asked how many are saved, this, too, is a question only God can answer. Whenever it was asked of Jesus, he immediately turned the question upon the questioner: "Strive to enter through the narrow door," Jesus exhorted the inquirer and his companions, though he also spoke of a broad road chosen by the many and a narrow road by the few (Luke 13:23ff.). The Book of Revelation depicts "a great multitude whom no man could count, from every nation, from all tribes and peoples and languages," praising God for salvation and indeed recognized as the redeemed (Revelation 7:9-17).

Clark Pinnock may well be on solid ground when he challenges the "fewness" doctrine, that is, the teaching that only a few will be saved. I also empathize with him when he draws back from an espousal of universalism.[22] Since I confess my ignorance about how many persons will be saved, obviously I am also agnostic about universalism. In addition to the principle stated above, namely, that it is presumptuous to make a judgment about the number saved, a judgment that only God can make, I also refuse to espouse universalism on the basis of my profound respect for human freedom. That is, it may well be that God has made us human beings with the kind of free wills that can ultimately oppose God and refuse the salvation that God offers through grace.

This seems to have been the view of Paul Tillich. Tillich believed in the possibility that human beings could ultimately refuse God's grace, a situation that would doom them to the self-destruction that actually means nonbeing. In this case, since by the refusal of the divine love people destroy themselves, both the freedom of the individual and the character of the divine love are preserved.[23]

However, certain passages, especially in the Pauline epistles, suggest universalism (Philippians 2:10-11; Colossians 1:19-20; and others). Moreover, if by some means unknown to me God chooses to save everyone, I certainly will raise no objection! Why do some persons, while professing to believe that salvation, including their own, is possible only through the grace of God, seem eager to see as many people as possible denied this saving grace?

The Nature of Judgment

And what is to be believed about eternal punishment? Many years ago, the late W. E. Hocking indicated not only that he rejected hell as a literal reality but that Christians generally agreed with him on this point. He suggested, however, that Christians had gone too far in lightening the gravity of moral decisions. He believed that "there is a moral equivalent of Hell; and the issues of life and death still hang on our moral decisions."[24] Surely Hocking was too optimistic in his assumption that Christians generally shared his view. Probably *liberal* Christians did, but not Christians in general. It is likely that even now most "evangelical" leaders, not to mention millions of conservative lay Christians, hold to the view of eternal torment. Many theologians, however, even those who are otherwise conservative, are espousing annihilationism, the view that some time after death unsaved persons cease to exist.[25] Tillich's view illustrates how a liberal theologian could believe in annihilationism. Tillich taught that judgment was the result of the individual's choice of nonbeing, and "nonbeing" is a kind of annihilation, is it not?

As for my own view, I have a profound problem with eternal torment as consistent with the character of a merciful, loving God. As is often remarked, how could God—or we Christians, for that matter—enjoy the bliss of heaven with the knowledge that many persons were eternally suffering? Would it be ethical to be in a place where God had wiped our tears away, had done away with death and had provided that "mourning and crying and pain will be no more" (Revelation 21:4), with the knowledge that many of our fellow human beings were enduring "mourning and crying and pain" forever? I think not.

I agree with Hocking that there is a "moral equivalent of Hell," that our moral decisions have grave consequences, but I am hard pressed to say specifically what those consequences are. I draw back from annihilationism, not just because it is difficult to support Biblically, but because it seems to indicate a failure on God's part to save some persons, a fact that is also true of the concept of eternal punishment. So I am caught between universalism, concerning which I have already said that I am agnostic, and a conviction that there is a "moral equivalent of Hell" which I find difficult to articulate beyond the belief that our moral decisions are of very great significance, a belief, by the way, that clearly implies God's judgment upon sin.

That God's holy character can in no way condone sin is a concept clearly taught in Scripture. "It is a fearful thing to fall into the hands of the living God" (Hebrews 10:31) is a Biblical teaching that I, for one, cannot set aside, though it is important to note that this sobering word from Hebrews—like so many Biblical references to judgment—is addressed to Christians.

God is certainly described in Scripture as perfect in righteousness and holiness. In the epistle to the Hebrews, it is stated that "our God is a consuming fire" (Hebrews 12:29), though it may well be that both the awe-inspiring holiness and the all-consuming love of God are meant. In any case, God is never called "righteousness" or "holiness" though John declares boldly that "God is love" (1 John 4:8; see also 4:16).

On the question of whether there is an opportunity to receive salvation after death, also, I must admit my ignorance—though I am aware that some will interpret these confessions of lack of knowledge as an indication either of my stupidity or my lack of faith! The great mercy of God and the assurance that God does not desire any to be lost suggest that a postmortem opportunity is likely. So also does that puzzling statement that after his death Jesus went and preached to the spirits in prison, those "who in former times did not obey. . . . so that, though they had been judged in the flesh as everyone is judged, they might live in the spirit as God does" (1 Peter 3:18-20; 4:6).[26] And, of course, there is the word of the Apostles' Creed that Jesus "descended into hades."

Concerning the fate of those who continue to defy God and refuse God's grace and salvation, I am content to leave this whole matter of the final judgment to God, assured that it will be taken care of in keeping with God's own character, in which I have utmost confidence. Meanwhile, I shall try to confirm my own "calling and election," so that I may find the way prepared for me into the eternal kingdom (2 Peter 1:10-11).

Surely, certain things can be affirmed about the judgment, none of which deny God's grace to persons who are not Christians: (1) There is no doubt that in Scripture judgment is represented as both fearsome and joyous. It holds terror for the wicked but humble jubilation for the redeemed. Indeed it *is* "a fearful thing to fall into the hands of the living God" (Hebrews 10:31). (2) We may expect surprises in the judgment. After all, Jesus taught, for example, that "many shall come from east and west and will eat with Abraham and Isaac and Jacob" in the messianic banquet of salvation, while "the heirs" are cast out into outer darkness (Matthew 8:9; see Luke 13:29). Though "the heirs" are obviously the Jews in Jesus' thought, is there any reason why this appellation should not be applied to Christians today? Then there is that strange parable of the judgment in Matthew 25:31-46, in which both those who are refused and those who are accepted are caught by surprise. One cause for astonishment may be that persons who are not Christians are included! In any case, there is the terrible threat of judgment for those who have neglected the poor. (3) It hardly behooves any of us to presume upon our salvation. If, in God's inscrutable grace and infinite love, one is numbered among the redeemed, this is a matter not for any pride but for profound and humble gratitude.

Salvation and the Other Religions

What about the role of the other religions in salvation? That the religions, Christianity included, have their dark sides can be easily documented. But are the religions other than Christianity at least provisional vehicles of salvation, serving that function until the Christian church arrives? Is the saved Hindu or Buddhist or Muslim or some other religious devotee saved by the "sacraments" of his or her own religion? If so, what about those who are saved somewhere out in the culture where they do not participate at all in the religion or religions of their society? By what vehicles or "sacraments" are they saved? These are difficult questions, for which I do not have ready answers.

Using the criteria of character that we usually employ in determining who is a Christian, or who is a good Christian, there are many within the other religions—and outside them—who seem to exhibit similar traits. This is neither to say that salvation is by human goodness nor that the preaching of the gospel makes no difference. I am only reporting what I believe to be a fact of my own experience. As I have already indicated, I do not presume to say how many are saved or specifically who are saved.

Salvation Through the Sacrifice of Christ

As a Christian, however, in spite of my lack of surety about certain matters having to do with salvation, I do not hesitate to express my conviction that salvation, wherever found, is made possible solely through what God has done in Jesus of Nazareth. There is a "once-for-allness" to the cross. Like the author to the Ephesians, I see the cross of Jesus Christ as a universal event that broke down the wall of partition between Jew and Gentile, thus creating out of the two one new humanity (Ephesians 2:11-22), and by extension demolishing all our walls of separation. I understand the cross as an occurrence that partakes both of history and eternity, an event both historic and cosmic. Since it involved God incarnate, it happened both to God and to a human being. Indeed, I view "the blood of the cross" as a cosmic sacrifice, by which God intends to reconcile all created things, not just human beings but the whole universe, to God (Colossians 1:19-20). So I expect that out of some final conflagration there will appear "new heavens and a new earth" (2 Peter 3:12-13). God intends the redemption of the entire universe, not its annihilation.

Obviously, when you think about it, the whole world lives by the sacrifice of life. If we are meat-eaters, countless animals are slaughtered for the sustenance of our lives. If we are vegetarians, even the lives of vegetables and life-containing seeds are sacrificed for food to sustain us. We human beings encroach upon the environments of living creatures, thereby in some cases causing the extinction of whole species. Microscopic creatures lose their lives continually, even when we are entirely unaware of it, so that we may live. Life feeds upon life, and without death no one can live in this world.

It is likely that the priesthood of the Hebrew people was specifically designed with this fact of the universal need for sacrifice in mind. All of the earth was holy as belonging to God, and no animal was to be eaten without a proper sanction upon its death. At the outset of Hebrew religion, the Hebrew word for "slaughter" was also the word for "sacrifice." All permissible killings of animals was sacrificial slaughter.[27] This concept of sacrifice probably influenced the covenantal language of Exodus 19 by which the whole nation of Israel is designated as God's priest. Apparently, this vocation of priest has reference not just to human society, but to "the whole earth," which in the context is expressly indicated as belonging to God (Exodus

19:3-6). If this interpretation is correct, the nation Israel was to exercise priesthood not only to the world of human inhabitants but to all of the created order, which was sacred. The "murder" of human beings was expressly prohibited by the sixth commandment and even the slaughter of animals was sacrificial.

This fact that no life is possible without the sacrifice of life is a very disturbing and morbid thought, is it not? Unless there is one sacrifice in which the Victim somehow identifies with the victims of all sacrifices, willing or unwilling—and the vast majority are unwilling—then human beings seem doomed to callousness or indifference, on the one hand, or to a profound disquiet, a deep sense of the tragic, on the other. But the word of the gospel is that there has been such a sacrifice, a cosmic sacrifice, a sacrifice involving the Creator God, a sacrifice without which no salvation is possible, so terrible and tenacious is the power of sin. By this sacrifice, not only is human sin atoned for and the way to forgiveness assured, but the whole universe, most of which seems unaware of sin but all of which bears the marks of decay and death, is to be redeemed (Romans 8:18-25). The universe is on its way, not to annihilation but to some breathtakingly wonderful, indescribable transformation by which it will become clear

> That nothing walks with aimless feet;
> > That not one life shall be destroyed,
> Or cast as rubbish to the void,
> > When God hath made the pile complete.[28]

Out of the disintegration of the present universe we look for the appearance of "new heavens and a new earth, where righteousness [justice] is at home" (2 Peter 3:13).

I realize, of course, that the Biblical concept of atonement is a many-splendored thing. I have described it above in terms of my own concept of cosmic sacrifice, which I consider Biblical. This intuition may be found, also, in the rich mythology of various cultures. This is not to suggest that the atonement may not be approached from other standpoints, especially from the Pauline concept of sin as being the tragic basis for the necessity of atonement. I, myself, take seriously this Pauline understanding and sometimes preach or teach from its perspective. Please note, also, that in the above discussion I claim that the sacrifice of Christ is made necessary because of the tragic and terrible fact of sin.

Nor do I mean to exonerate the perpetrators of sacrifice who at times are abysmally evil. They may find forgiveness freely, by God's grace, but only through sincere repentance and faith, just as did those who crucified Jesus (Acts 2:23, 37-38).

Whoever is saved, therefore, is saved through the redeeming work of God through Christ, the cosmic or universal Logos who is one with God. Salvation, wherever experienced, is made possible through the incarnate life, death and resurrection of Jesus Christ and by the faith which is the vessel in which this redemption that God has provided is received. Whether this happens through the other religions as salvific vehicles, I do not profess to know. That it does happen to some persons within the religions and to some outside all religions I am convinced.

But what about the Christian mission? Is a mission for us Christians still valid?

CHAPTER 4

The Christian Mission and Other Missions

LET ME INDICATE at the outset that what this chapter attempts is by no means a full-scale discussion of the Christian mission. It aims only to address those questions concerning mission that are raised by the new encounter of the religions. Moreover, though it has general reference, it has special meaning for the mission of Western Christians, of whom I am one.

THE CHRISTIAN MISSION: BASIC MOTIVE

Is there a Christian mission? If so, what is its basic motive?

The Complexity of the Question

Hardly any Christian, of whatever category of the Christian theology of religions suggested above, would propose that we abandon the Christian mission or deny its existence. Rather, the question is, how do we interpret mission?

For example, there are many pluralists who insist they are not giving up the mission of Christian faith. I have already called attention to the promotion of the Christian mission by Stanley J. Samartha, a noted Indian theologian and ecumenist who is also a pluralist who relativizes the Christian revelation. Paul Knitter also strongly affirms mission, but on the basis of a theological reconstruction that is pluralist and, in my judgment, reductionist.[1]

Obviously, for negativists, who believe that there is no hope of salvation for those who have never heard the gospel or that those who are saved may be rare exceptions, the motive for missions is clear. The motive is to offer eternal salvation to those who otherwise have no hope, or almost no hope, of receiving it otherwise. Though there may be some place for loving ministries to persons with various needs and for institutions to help meet those needs, and even for some social and political action to see that certain root causes of these needs are removed, the *basic* motive remains the same: to save souls. This view is often defended by such Biblical passages as Romans 10:14-17, and it is difficult to refute on Scriptural grounds. I differ with it upon the basis of the fact that the Bible is ambiguous on this point. I prefer to follow those passages that show that God's revelation is universal and brings the possibility of salvation to all, as I have discussed in the previous chapter.

For those, such as I, then, who believe that God may indeed confer eternal life upon some who have never heard the gospel, the question of motive is much more complicated. Why should Christian missionaries go at all if people may be saved for eternity without their witness?

The Character of God

In the first place, I believe that the Christian mission rests upon the solid, ultimate authority of the revelation of God—Father, Son, and Spirit—as a missionary God, not upon the negative conviction that most if not all people are lost if they do not hear the gospel. The Scriptures, from beginning to end, confront us with the reality of a God who is seeking all of us because God loves us infinitely. It is because of this immeasurable love that God has acted for our salvation in Jesus Christ.[2] As the late James S. Stewart put it:

> I am sure we need constantly to remind ourselves that the imperative of the Church's mission to the world today rests solidly upon the indicative of the mighty acts in the

Incarnation, the Cross and the Resurrection, and that the dynamic for our unaccomplished task is the accomplished deed of God.[3]

If God is indeed a missionary God who gives revelation to all peoples, and if the fullest light we mortals know is in Christ, surely we have a joyous urgency to a mission that communicates this good news.

The Power of the Gospel

Secondly, I believe it would be presumptuous to suggest that the gospel makes no difference. Many persons, from various cultural and religious backgrounds, testify that the Christian gospel has profoundly changed their daily lives in this world and has given them the bright hope of life eternal. In both these dimensions of salvation who knows but that some may have been saved who would not have been if they had not heard the gospel? After all, Paul speaks of the gospel as "the power of God for salvation to everyone who has faith" (Romans 1:16). If it is only through the saving action of God in Jesus of Nazareth that people obtain eternal life, then is it not presumptuous to say that the clear annunciation of the good news of that salvation makes no difference in the prospects of that eternal life? And is there not the possibility that some who never hear the gospel may be hardened through habitual sinning so that they finally reject the grace of God which would save them?

Making the Name Known

Similarly, it is to be expected that, all other things being equal—which probably they are not—persons who have received in their inner selves the grace of the universal Logos will be eager to hear his name and respond in faithful obedience. Those who do so respond are to be received with joyous gratitude. But what of those who do not so respond? Perhaps among them also are some who have been touched by the grace of God. It would be mistaken and presumptuous, would it not, to judge them as evil or mistaken. God only knows their hearts and God only is capable of judging them as to their eternal salvation.

God's New Order

Thirdly, the emphasis of Jesus was upon the kingdom of God, which I prefer to call "God's new order," that is, upon the achieving of justice, love, and peace "on earth as it is in heaven" (Matthew 6:10). He seemed to make little if any distinction between what Wilfred Cantwell Smith termed "mundane" and "cosmic" salvation[4]—what most of us would call "this worldly" and "other worldly" salvation. God's new order gives breathtaking dimensions to the missionary task. This new order always has to do with God's prior concern with the poor and needy, the victims of oppression and injustice. This is a fact of incalculable importance. It means that God's salvation is never merely other worldly. It always has to do with the redemption of persons and society in this world.

But God's new order includes even more. It embraces the whole environment, not just us human beings. The gospel is God's good news to the whole creation, promising that the creation will not be annihilated but transformed into the new creation of God's design, "new heavens and a new earth where righteousness [justice] is at home" (2 Peter 3:13).[5] Obviously, such an understanding of what God purposes has profound and far-reaching ecological implications for the Christian mission. This mission is to be concerned with all of life and the whole of the universe and not merely with individual and even societal salvation.

Grateful Loyalty

Finally, I believe that the basic motive for the Christian mission is grateful loyalty or loyal gratitude. Something so wonderful has happened in Jesus Christ that I must share it with the whole world. I am profoundly grateful and I must express my thankfulness. At the same time, I must be loyal to the One who has purchased me at so great a price and with such unchanging faithfulness. I have a Lord, a Master. I must tell the world about him.

THE CHRISTIAN MISSION: ESSENTIAL PRINCIPLES

The motive for missions, then, though somewhat complicated, is clear—at least to me. But what about the underlying principles by which the Christian mission operates?

Humility

Let me state again that humility cannot be over-emphasized. Humility has always been necessary to the execution of the Christian mission, but Western missionaries could sometimes get by without an adequate supply of it in the colonial world of yesterday. We cannot do so in this postcolonial era. The Western and non-Western nations—or many today would use the terminology of Northern and Southern nations—for the most part represent contrasts of economic power. The Northern nations are often viewed as economic imperialists, but Christians cannot afford to add to this burden theological imperialism as well. Indeed, they must counteract both of these charges of imperialism.

Humility means, among other things, a profound respect for the culture and the people among whom the missionary works, whether he or she is a professional missionary sent from abroad or a Christian of the culture involved. While my family and I were in India for a year, on a trip to South India we were befriended by an Indian Christian layman. This man was greatly concerned that we lived in Varanasi (Banaras), an ancient city holy to Hindus, that of all places we spent Christmas there, and that I was studying Indian religions. He greatly feared that we were converting to Hinduism, and he was dogged in his attempts to save us from the wiles of that religion, which in his eyes was nothing but evil. Though his own religious and cultural background was Hinduism, he had absolutely nothing positive to say about that faith. With such an attitude, how could he have had any affirmative effects in his attempts to witness to Hindus?

Since religions are such important aspects of culture, the missionary's attitude toward them and their adherents is of special significance. One of the rules by which the missionary fulfills her or his responsibility is to speak only respectfully of the religion or religions of the people among whom he or she lives and works. (Of course, not to condemn obvious wrong in another religion is difficult, and I do not mean to ignore that problem. I am merely reserving it for another context.)

At this point, I am recalling an experience I had as a missionary in Japan; whether the context was evangelism or pastoral care or both I am not sure. My wife and I had treasured a relationship with a family for about thirty years. We had been present at the couple's marriage and at other important occasions. We had watched their four children grow to adulthood, and, from a distance, had been aware that the husband's parents had died. The wife and her widowed mother were Christians. The husband, an only son, was a Buddhist, as had been his deceased parents.

Though this family lived at some distance from us, the husband was now admitted to the cancer center of a hospital in our city. The wife requested that I visit him regularly and read Scripture and have prayer with him. She exacted from me the promise that I would not reveal to him that he had inoperable abdominal cancer. Her husband's doctor participated in this charade, pretending that the surgery that had revealed the inoperable cancer was the removal of a large part of the patient's stomach for ulcers and that he would soon recover. Of course, I received the sick man's consent for these Christian ministries, and he seemed genuinely grateful for my attempts to express Christian love and minister to him from my understanding of the gospel. I was sure that he knew as well as I that he was dying—after all, he was in a cancer center! Nevertheless, I had to choose my Scripture and construct my prayers very carefully so as not to suggest the gravity of his situation. At one point, after my prayer, he made the sign of the cross, for my eyes only. I felt a special bond with this good man in his dying.

After a few weeks of critical illness, he apparently had a remission of his cancer and returned home to resume the responsibilities of his business. Soon, however, he was back at the cancer center, and in spite of the fact that I rushed to see him as soon as I heard the news, I arrived only in the final moments of his earthly life to pray over his seemingly unconscious body as he died.

His wife then asked me to participate in his funeral, as one of about a dozen people with various relationships to this prominent business man. Each of us was to give a farewell message *(chohji)* directed to the deceased, facing his chrysanthemum-bedecked picture. The same custom, with which I was quite familiar, would have been followed had this man received funeral rites in a Christian church. What was different in this case was that the ceremony was conducted in a True Pure Land Buddhist temple, where the chanting Buddhist priests were in charge. I prepared my brief message with great care, so as not to offend my Buddhist hosts and at the same time offer comfort to the Christian wife, her family, and other mourners. I spoke to the deceased as though he were present with the Lord—which I believed to be the case—without specifically identifying the Lord as the Christian Christ or the Buddhist Amida. I felt that I had maintained my Christian integrity and yet had shown respect for a religion other than my own.

Of course, humility also means deferring to the churches that exist in the cross-cultural situation where the missionary serves. Kosuke Koyama has contrasted the "crusading mind" with the "crucified mind."[6] We most effectively disavow the imperialistic mind-set by assuming the role of a servant. Westerners need to be especially careful at this point. I have said elsewhere that "the controlling interest of missionary work in any country must not be in the hands of foreigners."[7] Humility is not easy, but it is absolutely essential.

Incarnation

Closely related is a second principle, that of incarnation. The Apostle Paul recognized this principle in the example of Jesus. He cited the beautiful hymn of Philippians 2:5-11 (whether he was the author of the hymn has not been determined):

> Let the same mind be in you that was in Christ Jesus,
> > who, though he was in the form of God,
> Did not regard equality with God
> > as something to be exploited,
> But emptied himself, taking the form of a slave,
> > being born in human likeness.

> And being found in human form,
>> he humbled himself
> And became obedient to the point of death—
>> even death on a cross.
> Therefore God also highly exalted him
>> and gave him the name that is above every name,
> So that at the name of Jesus every knee should bend,
>> in heaven and on earth and under the earth,
> And every tongue should confess that Jesus Christ is Lord,
>> to the glory of God the Father.

Undoubtedly, incarnation was the principle upon which Paul himself operated. He summed up his having become as Jews, Gentiles and others, by writing "I have become all things to all people, that I might by all means save some. I do it all for the sake of the gospel. . . ." (1 Corinthians 9:22-23). Just as Jesus had entered into our world in the incarnation, so the Apostle entered into the world of all to whom he ministered.

Here is the most important rule for the missionary: to enter fully into the world of other people, including their language, their culture, their history, and especially their religious life in order that from that inner perspective the missionary can communicate the gospel. No doubt this is what John Mackay meant by "winning the right to be heard."[8] And, in spite of the fact that Hendrik Kraemer may be criticized for too much of a hard line toward the other religions, it is difficult to fault him when he affirmed this principle. In discussing the then current "points of contact" question of dialectical theology, Kraemer wrote:

> Only a genuine and continuous interest in the people as they are creates real points of contact. . . . As long as a man feels that he is the object of interest only for reasons of intellectual curiosity or for purposes of conversion, and not because of himself . . . in his total empirical reality, there cannot arise that humane natural contact which is the indispensable condition of all real religious meeting. . . .[9]

Surely, to go as a missionary to people about whose culture, including their religion or religions, one knows nothing, will be viewed as an insufferable arrogance that Christians cannot afford.

Dialogue

Thirdly, there is the closely related dialogical principle of communication (which I shall discuss more fully in the next chapter). Monologue is imperialistic. Dialogue is incarnational. Far more important than formally planned dialogue sessions is dialogical communication in which one listens before speaking and while speaking. In public presentations that are dialogical—though the form may be monological—the listener is able to perceive whether she or he has already been heard by the speaker, which is to say that all missionary communication must be dialogical.

Paul Knitter goes farther. He writes that "mission *is* dialogue."[10] I prefer to say that the dialogical principle should determine missionary attitudes and approaches, while insisting that mission itself is broader and more inclusive than dialogue. Mission also involves proclamation, efforts to preserve and improve the environment, to right relations with other religions, to serve the poor, and to engage in social and political action.

Confessionalism

A fourth principle is that the communication of the Christian message is of the nature of testimony. It is confessional. Jesus himself told his disciples that they were to be "witnesses," and he insisted that their witness was to be empowered by the Holy Spirit (Luke 24:48; Acts 1:8). They later insisted that they could only testify to what they had "seen and heard" (Acts 4:20). Whether we are communicating the gospel by word, deed, and very life or giving it a theological interpretation, our communication is a testimony to our faith in the living God who has come to us in Jesus of Nazareth. It is nothing if not empowered by the Holy Spirit. Indeed all the principles suggested above, humility, incarnation and dialogue, as well as confessionalism, are dependent upon the indwelling power of the Holy Spirit.

The Christian message is not self-evident truth, nor is it scientific fact which can be proved. Our witness cannot run roughshod over the beliefs of other persons and impose itself upon them. We have no right to make Christians out of people whether they wish to be Christians or not. Nor do we have the authority to judge people as evil and deserving of punishment because they do not accept our message. The gospel expects the response of faith, not the well-nigh inevitable assent demanded by self-evident fact. And faith must always be free, our faith and everyone's faith. If it is in any way coerced, is it faith at all? God alone is the final judge of a person's response, and we do well to leave judgment to God.

The confessional principle does not mean a mere fideism. It is not faith simply for the sake of faith. I believe that our faith is based upon some solid historical facts: the revelation of the Bible in its totality, centering in the crucial events of the life, death, and resurrection of Jesus Christ. But there is no way to prove the Christian claims concerning these events. For example, we may *claim* that the historical fact of the death of Jesus means eternal and universal redemption for the universe, but we have no way of proving this claim, regardless of how firmly we may believe it.

Interreligious Cooperation

A fifth principle is that of interreligious cooperation. Churches are familiar with the more limited practice of *ecumenical* expressions of unity and cooperation within the Christian circle, however poor and inadequate these expressions may be. Ecumenism may well go beyond the Christian denominations and be truly interreligious. However, I shall reserve that discussion for the next chapter when I write about interreligious relationships. Suffice it to say here that cooperation with the other religions in attacking the basic ills of society is fully warranted and, as I see it, mandatory. It is one part of the Christian mission.

The Relevance of the Church Growth Ideology

Finally, what about Church Growth principles? Do they have any relation to the development of a theology of religions? (I discuss this ideology only because it is so prominent in missiological circles today.) A preliminary question is what are the basic principles of the Church Growth missiology? According to the founder of this school of thought, the late Donald A. McGavran, the principles are three: (1) God intends or wills church growth, and church growth therefore is a "chief and irreplaceable goal [or purpose][11] of Christian mission." (2) Church growth occurs best in "receptive units" of population, and receptivity is determined largely by statistical measurements. (3) Churches of "homogeneous" memberships grow much more naturally and rapidly than those of "conglomerate" memberships, since people like to become Christians without crossing cultural boundaries.[12]

While I recognize and appreciate certain values of the Church Growth school, I am critical of all these principles. However, I shall restrain myself and discuss this missiology only at the points of its relevance for the development of a theology of religions. Of particular significance here is the first of these principles which articulates the basic purpose or motive of the Christian mission. I believe that the "chief and irreplaceable purpose of the Christian mission" is not church growth but the faithful communication of the gospel of Christ, motivated by gratitude for the grace of God. There are situations where faithfulness in communication certainly will not result in statistical growth of churches.

There are priorities fully as important as a "receptive" population. Among these is the priority of an *unreceptive* area, particularly when the unreceptiveness has resulted, at least in part, because of the hostile and cruel behavior of Christians toward the people involved, as in the cases of Jews, Muslims, Native Americans, and others. These people represent a special priority for Christians, and, as I have already indicated, they must be approached in an attitude of deep humility and repentance. This priority of unreceptive people is closely related to the example of Jesus and the principle of the cross: Jesus steadfastly set his face toward Jerusalem and his execution. He did not turn to a more receptive place and people—although he certainly could have done so. There is also the priority of the Holy Spirit's leading, which is often quite mysterious and cuts across all human logic about where people and funds should be sent.

However, in this context, my chief criticism of the Church Growth ideology is that it tends to ignore the world religions or else to treat them cavalierly or negatively. In McGavran's largest and most comprehensive book on church growth, for example, "religion" or "religions" does not even appear in the index, though "a vast relativism, based on the study of non-Christian religions," is discussed negatively on two pages.[13] In a more recent and much smaller volume, McGavran similarly denounces religious relativism. However, in this context he indicates his approval of cultural adaptation and an "irenic approach" to the religions, the latter of which he does not clearly define. The discussion is more positive than that of his previous volume, but it comprises less than two pages, and the primary concern is Paul Tillich's idea of the *latent church*.[14]

Both motive and principles of mission, therefore, must be seriously rethought in light of the questions raised by a theology of religions. And the same must be said for the methods that are employed and the persons and places where missionaries are sent.

THE CHRISTIAN MISSION: METHODS OF OPERATION

By what methods should Christians share the meaning of Christian faith with persons of other religions—proclamation of the gospel? Christian presence? deeds of love? social and political action concerning basic human and ecological problems? dialogical discussions?

The Broad Scope of Missionary Methods

Perhaps all of the means I have identified above are relevant. The Christian mission should be conceived as broadly as possible because the gospel is concerned with all of life. It is not even limited to human life, since God and the gospel are concerned with the reconciliation of the whole universe to God. One of the basic challenges to Christians, in prayer for example, is to stretch our interests toward the universal concerns of

God. The Christian mission is directed to all of human culture, of course including the religions, and beyond.

Therefore, all the suggestions I have made by way of the questions above are valid aspects of the Christian mission. Some are more relevant in certain situations than others, and some in certain cultures will be impossible. Proclamation of the gospel—public preaching—is always appropriate if allowed and if it is done according to the dialogical principle I have discussed. Christian presence is also very significant and in some cases is the only method possible. For example, in some of the Muslim countries, not one word of Christian communication is permitted, and the silent presence of the Christian is the only witness that can be made. C. S. Song's reminder that the Christian presence must always be distinguished from Christ's presence is salutary. Song believed that in the history of Christianity up to now "Christian presence in the world has more often than not obscured the presence of Christ."[15] This is a sad commentary indeed. Here also is a place for recognition of the essential work of the Holy Spirit to make Christ's presence known.

Also, social and political action as an expression of the gospel is imperative, strengthened all the more if interreligious. However, there are situations where religious efforts at social justice and environmental improvement are impossible. Christians in China, for instance, are expected to support the revolutionary and reformatory ideals of the Communist regime and not to launch out on attempts to improve the world as an expression of Christian faith. But deeds of love are always essential to the communication of the gospel and can hardly be prohibited. Indeed, in China, as we know, Christianity persists and is growing rapidly, surely in some significant measure because of the loving witness of the lives of Christians.

When Religion Is Oppressive

In cases where a religion itself is oppressive and furthers injustice, it is very difficult for expatriate missionaries to criticize or condemn its wrongs, since they are usually considered guests of the country to which they have been sent. The situation today is very different from the former era of Western colonialism, in which, for example, William Carey and his British colleagues could join with certain Hindus, as well as British colonial authorities, in opposing the practice of *sati*, the burning of widows on their husbands' funeral pyres. This abhorrent practice was sanctioned by a corrupt Hinduism. In the postcolonial world of today, usually it is better to defer to national Christians to make the protests, though this method of dealing with the problem also is questionable. For example, it may appear that the missionary is evading responsibility because of cowardice. Of course, it is possible for the missionary to alleviate this problem by seeking to become a citizen of the country involved. Such sacrifices of citizenship for the sake of Christian faith are by no means unknown. In any case, individual missionaries must make their own judgments about how to relate to unjust practices on the part of religions, as well as governments and various other institutions.

The Method of Dialogue

I have already indicated that dialogue is a Christian missionary principle. But dialogue is not only a principle, it is also a method. Dialogue accepts the other as an equal and not as an inferior. Almost always disputations and debate are unsuccessful, whether done formally or in an unplanned way. The older practice of debate or argument, especially between Christians and Muslims, has largely been replaced by less confrontational methods such as dialogue. Both as principle and as method dialogue is of the greatest importance. As I shall point out in the next chapter, if dialogue is not evangelism, it certainly is an aid to evangelism.

THE CHRISTIAN MISSION: PERSONS AND PLACES

To whom and to where should missionaries be sent? And what kinds of missionaries?

Traditional Missions

There is still a place for traditional missions, in my judgment, but with certain qualifications. In places where the Christian church already exists, missionaries may serve an ecumenical function as representatives of another culture or another kind of Christianity. Western missionaries sent to such places, however, should be few, and missionary efforts should be directed toward the development and support of the national churches and their leaders. In addition, this should be a two-way and not a one-way street. We in America, not to mention other Western nations, very much need the ministry and witness of Christians from other countries to help us in our Christian tasks and to look more objectively at our cultural syncretisms. Indeed, we need the insights of Christians from other lands to aid us in developing a theology of religions. Always churches, wherever they exist, should be helped toward a wholesome indigenization and contextualization, which involves a vital relationship to their own religious heritage, without becoming captives to culture.

Unreached Peoples and Questions of Terminology

Secondly, I believe that Christian missionaries are justified in their emphasis upon sending missionaries to *unreached peoples*, though this emphasis is not without its difficulties, not the least of which is terminology. The term *unreached peoples* not only sounds patronizing, but people have a right to know what has not reached them. Is it God? revelation? truth? meaning? Most of them believe that they have indeed been reached by the Ultimate, and who can deny that God is present before the missionary arrives? The term *unreached peoples*, then, raises difficult ethical and theological as well as cultural questions. The term *frontier peoples*, which used to be heard more often than it is today, is likewise unacceptable. To suggest that people are on a frontier inevitably connotes a more primitive or backward or undeveloped culture than that of those using the term. *Hidden peoples*, likewise, has unfortunate implications, very similar to *unreached peoples*. Those called by this term might well ask, hidden from whom or from what?

An acceptable terminology is very difficult to decide upon, but, in my judgment, the terms discussed thus far, however meaningful they may be to Western Christians, should be forthrightly abandoned. I would prefer an out-and-out

Christian term such as *unevangelized*, though *evangelized* and *unevangelized* have come to have special meanings for Western missiologists.¹⁶ Apart from these special meanings, however, *unevangelized* means nothing more than *ungospelized*; that is it signifies a place or a people where the Christian message is not yet known or not yet well known. Possibly the terms *evangelized* and *unevangelized* could be used with some redefinition.

Problems of Misrepresentation

Apart from terminology, there is another ethical problem involved. I am told that those sent to "unreached peoples," particularly to countries where missionaries are not admitted or not welcomed, sometimes misrepresent themselves as specialists who have no relation to mission boards, though in fact they have been sent and are supported by mission boards. This is the kind of dishonesty that cannot be squared with Christian ethics. Only those who are in fact unrelated to mission agencies have the right so to represent themselves.

I have long advocated the great increase of "non-professional" missionaries, that is, persons with some kind of professional or technological skill that might be highly useful in some cultures. These persons would be Christians, employed by some nonreligious agency, of course, and not directly related to a missionary society, though one would hope that they would have definite missionary motivation. That kind of "non-professional" missionary is quite different from one whose identity is falsified. Christian evangelism can never afford to be less than thoroughly honest.

Similar problems obtain with regard to *nonresidential* missionaries, missionaries who live outside the country or region to which they are assigned and to which they make periodic visits. Such missionaries may misrepresent themselves in order to have access to Christian groups within a given country. Such practices cannot be condoned. In addition, nonresidential missionaries may be a source of embarrassment or danger to national Christians. To assume that one has to forsake truth to have access to people where missionaries are not admitted is both shoddy ethics and poor theology. Why should I suppose that God has no access to people unless some missionary is present? Is not God already there before Christians arrive? Even if, as I have suggested, the witness to the gospel makes a difference, is the difference sufficient to justify the setting aside of Christian ethics? Moreover, in almost all cases, at least a small community of Christians is present, and the nonresidential missionary, by the very fact that she or he does not live with these Christians, may escape the responsibility of really identifying with them. Therefore, the nonresidential missionary, whose ministry may well be valid in certain situations, needs to exercise great sensitivity and scrupulous honesty.

New and Bold Initiatives

While continuing the more traditional missions, therefore, and refining them to accord with new realities and ethical requirements, we may well consider new and bold initiatives. After all, with rare exceptions, we are only witnessing to our faith on the fringes of the religions, or to their nominal constituencies, and perhaps on the outskirts of the intellectual life of the world as well. Why not send missionaries who are specialists in certain religions to take up residence in the center of a religion, there to engage in dialogue, formal or informal, with religious leaders and theologians?

Jürgen Moltmann has suggested something resembling this proposal. In addition to traditional missionaries, wrote Moltmann, we might send missionaries whose specific aim would be to "infect" people of other religions with the Christian ideals of hope, love, and world responsibility. This qualitative mission, which Moltmann viewed as having taken place unconsciously in the history of Christian missions, should now be pursued with deliberate intent to encourage a climate in which the desperate problems of the world might be addressed. This kind of missionary would have the role of "critical catalyst."[17]

Some years earlier, Wilfred Cantwell Smith had made a similar recommendation. Smith suggested that missionaries do deliberately what for the most part they had been doing unwittingly and clumsily, namely, participate in the life and history of other religious communities. He suggested further that only those missionaries be sent who were acceptable to the leaders of those religious communities.[18] It seems to me that these proposals have merit and should be seriously considered by leaders of missionary agencies.

Whereas traditionally, in addition to evangelistic missionaries, we have sent specialists in education, medicine and agriculture, in light of the new discernment of environmental realities we need to give emphasis to another category, that of *missionary earthkeeper*. We are hardly scratching the surface of this new responsibility and opportunity. The care of the environment should be recognized as an important kind of missionary contribution. Not only could Christian earthkeepers help people of their own and of other religious faiths to be more effective environmental specialists, they could also profit from the insights of environmentalists of other religions, and from the attitudes of those other religions toward the environment, in making their own work more effective.[19]

Missions of Third World Christians

One other word needs to be spoken. The participation of Third World Christians in the international mission is of breathtaking importance for various reasons. In recent years we have come to know something of how large the numbers of these Third World missionaries have become. Some missiologists are even predicting that the Christian mission in the future will largely be executed by Third World Christians and that the efforts of Western Christian missions will be minimal. Though some missionaries from Third World churches carry on their missionary work across cultural boundaries, many others operate in their own or a similar culture, where the religious heritage is theirs. In either case, as they relate to these religious environments, no doubt they will help us to develop a more adequate and relevant theology of religions.

EVANGELISTIC EXPECTATIONS

Should Christians expect that persons of other religions will confess Jesus Christ as Lord? If such confessions occur, how should the new Christians relate to their own religious heritage—by complete rejection? by fulfillment in Christ? by critical selection: abandonment, retention and transformation?

Missions and the Confession of Christ

Surely if Christians believe that Jesus Christ is Lord, as the basic Christian baptismal confession avers, and if the meaning is the *universal lordship* of the Christ, then obviously Christians will expect that at least some of the adherents of other religions will join them in this confession. The Apostle Paul expected that eventually—perhaps eschatologically—"at the name of Jesus every knee should bend, in heaven and on earth and under the earth, and every tongue should confess that Jesus Christ is Lord, to the glory of God the Father" (Philippians 2:10-11). It is likely that Paul had only scant if any acquaintance with the great religions of Persia, India and China, though they had already been existing for several centuries.

Though we have much greater knowledge of the world religions than did Paul, is it unreasonable for us to take the same stance? I think not. What is of crucial importance is a thorough commitment to religious freedom and the following of the principles suggested above: profound humility, the incarnational principle, the confessional nature of the Christian witness, the dialogical method of communication, and interreligious cooperation.

New Christians and Their Religious Heritage

The question of how new Christians should relate to their religious heritage is somewhat complicated. The first thing to say is that they should have the freedom to do this relating themselves, under the leadership of the Holy Spirit, without missionaries breathing down their necks. To be sure, missionaries will often be asked to give advice on this question, and in such instances the counsel should be given with great tact and sensitivity, even reticence. Often such questions can be referred to a national Christian, especially a pastor. This is but one way the missionary can defer to national Christian leadership.

Sometimes new Christians feel so threatened by their religious environment that they opt to totally reject it. In such cases it may take a generation or two for them to effect some positive attitudes and relationships—even if the missionaries do not seek to influence them negatively. In other instances they are eager to relate their Christian faith to the religion of their environment.

Let me give a couple of examples from my missionary experience in Japan which may shed some light on this whole question of Christians relating to their religious heritage. One concerns a missionary colleague. Along with a Japanese seminary student, this missionary had responsibility for developing a new congregation of Christians, which in its beginnings met in his house. When the congregation grew large enough to have a building of its own, the missionary expressed his hope that the building would represent Japanese and not Western architecture. Much to his chagrin, the missionary discovered that he was overruled. The congregation feared that if a Japanese type of building were constructed it would resemble a Buddhist temple and not be distinctive as a Christian church. They preferred a structure that would, as they put it, express unity with Christianity in Europe and America. What they built resembled a small American church building, certainly not a Japanese building. (Of course, there are some Japanese churches that do indeed use not only a Japanese structure but also Japanese musical instruments, Japanese art, and the like. In my judgment, these churches should be applauded.)

The other illustration is from my own experience. After I had preached in a Christian evangelistic service in Nagasaki several years ago, a medical student sought me out to tell me that he was very much interested in becoming a Christian. His family were Buddhist, he said, and although he had no personal faith he had considerable respect for Buddhism. If he became a Christian, he asked me, would he need to reject what he believed was good and true in Buddhism?

I replied that I knew something about Buddhism and that I shared his respect for it. As I understood it, I told him, if he were to become a Christian, he would need to make clear his commitment. From now on Jesus would be Lord of his life. From the perspective of this new commitment he would survey his Buddhist heritage. I suspected, I told him, that much of this heritage would be retained, some would be abandoned and still other aspects would be transformed in meaning and value. Implied in what I said, I trust, was the likelihood that his Buddhist heritage would significantly influence his Christianity. Maybe I should have made that point more specific. I never knew whether he became a Christian. If so, no doubt he retained much of his Buddhist heritage and found it to be compatible with his new commitment to Christ.

OTHER RELIGIONS AND THEIR MISSIONS

Does God have a mission for the other religions? If so, what is it, and how should Christians understand and relate to it?

Other Religious Missions and Questions of Fairness

I have already indicated that although terminology may vary, most any religion has some sense of purpose, some awareness of vocation, some conviction about its *raison d'etre*. It may not use the term *mission*, since mission is a Christian term, but it has some corresponding sense of its responsibility. Some religions, notably Baha'i, Buddhism, and Islam, are clearly missionary faiths. Others, such as most varieties of Hinduism, though believing in the basic equality and validity of all religions and the inappropriateness of missionary efforts on the part of any, nevertheless have a conviction concerning the Ultimate and of something they possess that is worth sharing with the world, even if it is the conviction that no religion should do anything that savors of missionary activity! In this understanding, all religions, from the Christian standpoint, have some sense of mission.

Some Christians have been saying for a long time that the Christian mission is not the only mission God has in the world. God has a mission for other religions as well. Wilfred Cantwell Smith was saying it many years ago.[20] More recently, S. J. Samartha stated it similarly. "If Christians speak of 'mission,'" said Samartha, "they must be willing to recognize that their "neighbors too have their 'missions' in the same pluralistic world."[21] It may be indeed that God has a mission for other religions. Who am I to say that God does not?

If so, what is the Christian to say about the missions of the other religions? In the first place, there should be scrupulous fairness in our relationships, should there not? If I expect Christian missionaries to have freedom to live and work and give their witness abroad, then I should be willing for others to have the same privileges in our society. This is a simple matter of the Golden Rule, to treat others as one would wish to be treated. Fairness means also that if I expect missionaries to have access to young people of other faiths, I should be willing for the young people of my religion to be accessible to the missionary efforts of others. I am well aware that children may be vulnerable and impressionable and may need some shielding from certain missionary approaches, but if this is the case, then I should exercise the same sensitivity toward the children of others as I wish others to practice toward my children. If Christians insist that we have the truth and therefore should protect our own rights and not those of others, I reply that adherents of other religions also believe that *they* have the truth. What I am advocating is nothing but fairness.

Secondly, persons of any religion should have the right to define their own mission, that is, their own understanding of their religion's purpose for being. No one of another faith has a right to define it for them. In the next chapter, in the discussion of Christianity's relation to Judaism, I shall insist that Christians should define their own mission and that Jews should do the same for their faith. This freedom of definition I take to be a universal principle that all should respect.

The Necessity for Religious Freedom

What I am pleading for in both of the above suggestions is religious liberty. My own nation, the United States of America, professes to believe in this ideal and our Constitution provides for it. In the situation of growing religious pluralism in our society, religious freedom seems to be in real danger. The call of the religious right for a "Christian nation" seems to mean a nation in which the Christian religion, as understood by Christian rightists, is preferred. Important political offices are to be occupied by conservative Christians, official prayers of some sort are to be permitted in the schools, the teaching of science and history is to be determined by doctrines of Christian rightists, and the character of the nation is to be identified with what certain conservative Christians interpret to be the will of God.[22] Although I am convinced that persons of all religious and nonreligious views have the right to engage fully in politics, these efforts of the religious right are profoundly disquieting and must be resisted. Majority religions, particularly, must be extremely sensitive to the religious rights of people of other faiths. If not, real religious freedom in the United States is in severe jeopardy.

CHAPTER 5

Interreligious Relationships

THE NEXT QUESTION has to do with how Christians should relate to persons of other religions. I have already discussed the Christian mission to other religions and the recognition of the missions of the various religions. Missionary activity, of course, is one kind of interreligious relationship; and, conversely, rightly relating to the religions is a part of Christian mission. In a sense, therefore, the question I am raising here is but an extension of the previous question of mission. In addition to what I have already said about mission, then, how else should religions relate to each other—by interreligious dialogue, by cooperation, by interreligious worship, by all of these?

MODES OF INTERRELIGIOUS RELATIONSHIPS

Interreligious Dialogue

Development. Dialogue between persons of different religions is almost entirely a phenomenon of the latter half of the twentieth century. Until that time, intercourse between religions was usually a form of apologetics. That is, a religious representative tried to establish the superiority of her or his particular religion. When the newly emerging science of the study of world religions began to bring people together across religious lines, the conversations were usually between individuals. Even interreligious conferences resulting from the new interest in religions, such as the World Parliament of Religions of 1893, usually meant religious representatives taking turns at monologue.

The religions were not really meeting each other; they were more like ships passing each other in the night. Thus, the late Hendrik Kraemer was prophetic when he called attention to "the *coming* dialogue of world cultures and world religions."[1] In 1960, when Kraemer made this claim, dialogue as a major activity of religious people was not very far advanced. However, study centers were already being established in various parts of Asia and Africa with the purpose of *in situ* study of the religions by Christians and the development of interreligious dialogue. These centers were related to the International Missionary Council and then to its successor, the Division of World Mission and Evangelism of the World Council of Churches. Some of these centers have been quite successful in accomplishing their purpose. Later, the World Council, through its Faith and Order Commission, accomplished a rather remarkable feat of developing interreligious dialogue, especially through the leadership of Dr. Stanley J. Samartha of India. By now, official dialogues between adherents of the various religions have become rather common, though Christian initiative has been prominent.

In addition, interreligious dialogue was occurring in relation to the study of world religions in universities. Perhaps the best example is the Center for the Study of World Religions at Harvard University. However, in addition to what was transpiring at Harvard, many teachers of world religions were involving themselves and their students in interreligious dialogue.

<u>Barriers.</u>   The development of dialogue has not been without controversy. From the Christian side, there are those who fear that the evangelistic motive will be abandoned for the sake of dialogue and that relativism or syncretism will result. Adherents of the other religions have often feared that dialogue is but a subtle or underhanded way of Christians trying to convert them.

Real dialogue, of course, does not promise to be easy. This is apparent from the rather famous definition by Reuel Howe:

> Dialogue is that address and response between persons in which there is a flow of meaning between them in spite of all the obstacles that normally would block the relationship. It is that interaction between persons in which one of them seeks to give himself as he is to the other, and seeks also to know the other as he is.[2]

The barriers to the dialogical relationship between religions are formidable: for example, at best there are the deep differences between religions, the passion that accompanies religious commitment, and the esoteric nature of religious experiences and religious language. In addition, Westerners obviously have an advantage over others in that the language of dialogue is almost always English, not to mention the fact that there are still vestiges of colonialism and economic if not political advantages enjoyed by Westerners. Some scholars have doubted that real interreligious dialogue is possible.[3] Others believe that true dialogue is impossible unless one adopts a pluralistic attitude.[4] One of the intentions of this book is to show that dialogue is possible for nonpluralist Christians without an imperialistic or a Christianity-centered attitude. Indeed, it can be argued that a pluralistic view, insofar as it relativizes Christology and Trinity, makes *Christian* dialogue impossible, since in that case the pluralist has already forsaken a traditional and, in my judgment, essential Christian claim for the sake of dialogue.

<u>Assumptions.</u> The difficulties of dialogue make it imperative that there be some assumptions accepted by the parties to the dialogue. The first of these is the presupposition of a common humanity that all persons share. The most obvious requirement is the use of a common language or interpretations into languages understood by all. This commonality goes deeper than ordinary speech, however, for religious language often reflects the profound, subtle and esoteric nuances of faith. Of course, a large part of the articulating, clarifying, and refining of definitions will have to be done in the process of dialogue itself.

Even where the Christian conviction of the human being created in the image of God is not shared by other dialogue partners, it must be assumed that in all religions there is a deep desire to find meaning in human existence. There is a capacity in rational, intelligent persons by which a significant measure of interreligious understanding between them is possible. It is this common humanity that provides the basis for dialogue.

A second presupposition that makes interreligious dialogue possible is respect for the other's religious convictions, even if one radically disagrees with them. There are profound differences in the beliefs of major religions, and it is not helpful to ignore them. The Theravadin Buddhist, for example, may well believe that there is no personal deity, only the ultimate experience of Nirvana. Yet he is convinced that in the teachings of Buddha he has found the way of salvation. Obviously, the Christian cannot agree with the Buddhist theologically. Nevertheless, there is profundity to the insights of Theravada and a tenacious attempt to preserve and follow the teachings of the Buddha himself, which the Christian may well respect.

It would seem much more appropriate to ask for mutual respect than for a shared theological conviction as the basis for dialogue. Even if the Christian does not believe, at least initially, that the faith of his or her partner in dialogue is the result of revelation—a Christian term not ordinarily used by representatives of South and East Asian religions—the Christian can respect the religious convictions of the other on the basis of their common humanity. Thus Christians can agree at least with the initial part of the admonition of the late M. A. C. Warren, that the first requisite for approaching another's religion is to remove your shoes, lest you thoughtlessly trample on someone's dreams.[5]

A third condition for interfaith dialogue is that each party to the dialogue be prepared to represent his or her own religion with knowledge and conviction, so that the dialogue may be a serious confrontation.[6] In addition, then, to basic knowledge and commitment to one's own faith, some reflection upon its content and meaning is appropriate as a preparation for dialogue. This requirement does not mean necessarily that the Christian must carefully select each item of creedal baggage before embarking on the journey into dialogue. Nor does it mean, in the case of Christians, that only seminary graduates have the credentials to engage in interfaith discussions. Lay persons, too, may be qualified, but only on the basis of careful, intelligent study of their religion. To know what one believes and to be ready to give an answer concerning one's fundamental hope (I Peter 3:15) is essential.

In the fourth place, for meaningful dialogue between persons of differing religions, some knowledge of the other's religion is important, though each party should have the freedom to define her or his own faith. The dialogue itself is designed to further mutual knowledge. Nevertheless, time can be spent more efficiently if it does not have to be used for elementary explanations of what each believes. Besides, in some cases, dialogue will be planned to bring the perspective of the different faiths to bear upon some common issue, such as population control or world peace. If so, an elementary knowledge of the other's faith will permit focusing upon the issue for discussion without long excursions into explanations.

Assumed knowledge of a religion to which one is not committed can be deceiving. One may find that what one *thinks* are the tenets of another's faith are not at all what this religion believes and teaches. For all this, some basic knowledge of the other's faith, subject to correction in dialogue, is certainly preferable to none.

A final presupposition is the willingness to take the risks that interreligious dialogue involves. Authentic dialogue requires both parties involved to be open to criticism of their most cherished beliefs without taking offense. It requires that they be willing to subject their basic convictions to serious challenge. In dialogue one must reckon with the fact that the conversations may result in a change in religious allegiance, either one's own or that of a partner in dialogue. So the risks are rather formidable. Dialogue is not for the fainthearted!

Lesslie Newbigin has stated that the experience of dialogue serves to judge and correct one's own Christianity and expose its disobedience hidden behind the appearance of obedience. "Each meeting with a non-Christian partner in dialogue therefore," says Newbigin, "puts my own Christianity at risk."[7] In another place in the same essay, Newbigin states even more emphatically the Christian's vulnerability in dialogue:

> ... we are vulnerable.... We do not possess the truth in an unassailable form. A real meeting with a partner of another faith must mean being so open to him that his way of looking at the world becomes a real possibility for me. One has not really heard the message of one of the great religions that have moved millions of people for centuries if one has not been deeply moved by it, if one has not felt in his soul the power of it.[8]

<u>The Christian Purpose.</u> Lesslie Newbigin also indicated that for the Christian the purpose of dialogue "can only be obedient witness to Jesus Christ." However, he states further that its purpose is not "that Christianity should acquire one more recruit."[9] That is, the purpose of dialogue is not, at least immediately, an evangelistic intention.

It is important to notice that many others, like Newbigin, insist that the Christian must not, for the sake of dialogue, sacrifice central Christian convictions. An example is the Anglican theologian John V. Taylor, who insists that what God did in Jesus Christ, particularly in the cross, was necessary for the salvation of all persons everywhere. And he believes that "this *kind* of statement" is appropriate for dialogue, whether coming from Christians or from adherents of other religions. Taylor thinks that all religions have their "jealousies," that is, points at which the adherents of any faith, even religions such as Hinduism and Buddhism, must by necessity believe that their own faith has universal finality. And to Taylor, this fact is not at all objectionable. So the believers of each religion must lay their absolutes out for others to see and then to listen carefully and honestly to the critique that others will give to these irreducible claims.[10]

So Taylor speaks primarily of "claims" that the Christian makes in dialogue. Unlike Newbigin, he does not speak of dialogue as a form of witness. Though it seems to me that the two mean very much the same, Taylor's tone is much softer than Newbigin's. However, in a later discussion, Newbigin indicated that the essential contribution of the Christian to dialogue is simply the telling of the story of Jesus.[11] It seems to me that this is a much better way to express it. Even so, I would prefer to use the term "confess"—in dialogue the Christian confesses her or his faith. "Confess" is a less threatening word than "witness." Probably the term "witness" should not be used in dialogue, in spite of the fact that it is a perfectly good Christian—and Jewish—word, used by Jesus (Acts 1:8, quoting from Isaiah 43:10,12).

If, with Newbigin, we use the word "witness" in the context of dialogue, would it not be better to say that the Christian's purpose in dialogue is to become *a more effective witness* for Christ by understanding truly what others believe and feel? This way of putting it preserves Newbigin's emphasis upon witness while leaving some room for the openness and vulnerability that he also strongly affirms. To say that the purpose of dialogue itself is "obedient witness to Jesus Christ" may evoke images of a psychologically coercive Christian evangelism, which Newbigin certainly does not sanction but of which Christians are too often guilty. Frequently fears of this kind of evangelism are serious hindrances to dialogue.

I believe that Taylor is right about the "jealousies" held by each religion. If so, then it is foolish for Christians, for the sake of authentic dialogue, to pretend that Christian faith makes no such claims to finality. It is much more appropriate to put these claims on the table for careful scrutiny by the partners in dialogue, as Taylor suggests.

If representatives of other religions tend to suspect that dialogue disguises an evangelistic purpose on the part of Christians, the latter, along with Jews and Muslims, are more likely to be afraid of syncretism. In a little booklet published by the World Council of Churches and entitled *Guidelines on Dialogue with People of Living Faiths and Ideologies*, there is a forthright discussion of syncretism. The booklet recognizes the unfortunate truth that almost inevitably the word *syncretism* is used with negative connotations; but the little book acknowledges that whether one uses the term or not, there are certain dangers in dialogue at this very point. One is that in the attempt to "translate" the Christian faith in various cultural settings, the Christian in dialogue "may go too far and compromise the authenticity of Christian faith and life." A second danger is that of interpreting another faith not on its own terms but in terms of one's own faith or ideology. It is significant that Western Christians who are most fearful of syncretism usually ignore how much their own Christianity has accommodated itself to Western culture.[12]

<u>The Results.</u> What may we expect from interreligious dialogue? What fruits will it produce? In the first place, unless in the process of dialogue one has succumbed to the appeal of another faith and embraced it—which, if the dialogue is truly honest, is always a live possibility—it may be expected that dialogue will facilitate mutual understanding. Many Christians have testified that in participating in dialogue with persons of other faiths they have come thereby not only to a better understanding of other religions but also of their own faith as well. That is, the other religions really have something to contribute to Christianity without which it is incomplete.

On the basis of my own limited experience in interreligious dialogue, I can give the same testimony. I have lived among adherents of Shinto, Buddhism, Hinduism, and Islam, and have engaged in personal conversations with some of them as well as with Jains, Sikhs, and Jews. In addition, I have participated in some planned dialogues among Christians and representatives of certain other religions. Through these experiences, I have not only acquired a better understanding of these religions, I have also come to know and appreciate my own faith at a broader and more profound level.

Secondly, this process, by which the religions in their hidden depths come within the range of Christian perception and vice versa, may give us insights into how the Christian faith may truly be contextualized or indigenized in the different cultural settings of the world. If so, dialogue will help fulfill the Christian mission through which the Christian faith itself comes into the fullness of its universality—as the nations of the earth with their diverse cultures and religions pour their treasures into the eternal City of God (Revelation 21:24-26).

In the third place, while Christian participation in dialogue is never to be confused with evangelism, as we have stated earlier, it nevertheless provides a context and suggests a method for evangelism. On the one hand, when formal dialogue is planned between Christians and adherents of other faiths, these non-Christian partners in dialogue need assurance that the conversations are for mutual sharing of knowledge and insights and not for the purpose of propagandizing and trying to convert. On the other hand, it needs to be understood, also, that Christians believe that Jesus Christ is Lord of the universe and that they cherish the hope that all persons will recognize him as such, whether this experience of acknowledging his authority is called "conversion" or not.

The question of conversion is a complex one and the term itself is loaded. Once upon a time a distinction could be drawn between *conversion* and *proselytism*, but now the two terms carry much of the same meaning and much of the same opprobrium. We Christians need to search for other terminology to prevent unnecessary offense in our missionary relationships.

Perhaps the real difficulty is not the fact that Christians seek to evangelize others but the way we go about it. Certainly the attempt to make someone over after my own image is obnoxious and prideful and cannot be squared with Christian ethics. However, to hope that others may share with me the incomparable blessings of the universal gospel, which is no more mine than theirs, to hope that in the fullness of human freedom they may acknowledge the Christ who asserts his gracious authority over all of life and to hope that they will hold and develop this faith in ways consonant with their own culture—surely to hold this hope and to act in accordance with it is Christian.

Moreover, an authentic experience of faith in Christ, when it occurs, is a work accomplished by the Holy Spirit and not by human beings as such; and it is a commitment to Christ and his church and not to a mere human structure. Especially is it important to recognize that we have no right to seek to control the Christ as he is understood and manifested among others whose culture differs from ours. Human beings must have the freedom of faith, and the Christ must be—and indeed is—both free and sovereign.

Dialogue, then, can help us to understand the true meaning of evangelism. In the deeper and broader sense, Christian evangelism is always dialogical. True evangelism is confession of one's own faith, proceeding from love by the method of empathy, entering into the world of others, walking down the road with them, listening to them talk, becoming "all things to all persons" in order "by all means to save some" (1 Corinthians 9:22). It seeks to help the other to know Christ and to decide concerning him, but it will not coerce or manipulate that decision, psychologically or otherwise.

As I have suggested previously, dialogue is communication between equals, not between superior and inferior. Monological witness implies superiority and imperialism. Dialogical witness depends upon the convincing power of the Truth who is the unseen party in the dialogue. Perhaps interreligious dialogue will enable us to think and speak dialogically rather than monologically as we seek to fulfill our missionary task. If so, it should help to free us from the effect of several centuries of Western imperialism and paternalism, which has tragically impeded our evangelism in the non-Western world. I reiterate for emphasis that our speaking should always give evidence that we have listened to those to whom we are addressing the gospel before we have presumed to speak to them.

Maybe the deep searching for truth across religious and cultural lines, which interreligious dialogue provides, will give us insights into how persons in the context of African and Asian cultures, in the vast reaches of the Buddhist, Hindu, and Muslim worlds, may become Christians without the apparent loss or truncation of their indigenous cultures. How may Christianity be truly indigenized, or contextualized? This is a question about evangelism, and it is of immeasurable importance.

Finally, there is some promise that dialogue between Christians and persons of other religious commitments will show ways to cooperate in active measures toward building a better society and a better world. But this subject deserves separate treatment.

Interreligious Cooperation

Surely there is a place for interreligious cooperation in confronting the grave problems that beset the human race. C. S.

Song has said that a fundamental task of the Christian church in Asia is that of Christians working together with Asians of differing religions and ideologies "to transform Asian society on the basis of freedom, justice, and equality."[13] Such working together in partnership gives opportunity for Christians to give witness to the liberating character of God's new order as we understand it, while those of other faiths are free to represent the liberating aspects of their own faith according to their own understanding.

Areas of Cooperation. One natural area of interreligious cooperation is the pursuit of religious freedom. It would be a great boon, indeed, if all religions would cooperate to see that everyone has religious liberty. Whether physical or psychological, coercion and manipulation have no place in religion.

After the first three centuries of its history, during which it was persecuted by Jews and by Romans, Christianity allied itself with political power and became itself the persecutor of Jews and others who were not Christians. It is especially at this point of religious freedom that there are terrible blots on our history: coerced conversions, crusades against Muslims and Jews and even against fellow Christians, inquisitions and roughshod violations of certain cultures.

I belong to a Christian denomination (Baptist) that has emphasized the necessity of religious and other freedoms and has made very significant contributions to Christianity and to Western history in this regard. However, in at least two ways my own awareness of this fact and my pride in bearing the name "Baptist" is modified: (1) Sometimes there are people who claim to be Baptists who are theologically coercive and do not really believe in freedom. (2) Even if my denomination had always been faithful to its conviction of religious liberty, which it has not, I would still confess my solidarity with all Christians and share their sense of guilt and repentance for the shameful aspects of Christianity's history, which is also my own history, although my own denomination did not begin before the seventeenth century.

Full religious freedom recognizes the inviolability of the citadel of conscience. It includes not only the right to believe in religion but also to reject religion and to give witness to this rejection. It insists upon the liberty both to believe and practice one's faith and also to propagate it. It means the right to retain one's own culture and not to have it violated or obliterated by someone's religious zealotry. I rejoice in the fact that in my own country, in spite of tenacious religious prejudices, and in spite of the violence done to the cultures of Native Americans, not only members of my own religion but also persons of other religious faiths have a very large measure of freedom to live and move and have their being. But, as I have indicated, this measure of religious liberty is now under threat.

Religious freedom means that every religion has the right to fulfill its own mission or whatever it may consider its major purpose in the world. As I have suggested previously, though terminology varies, surely all religions have some sense of mission that is probably part of their essence. Therefore, I reiterate that it would be a great advantage to the human race if persons of religious faith could agree to stand for freedom.

A second area of possible cooperation among religions is the ethical and spiritual service of humanity. All religions claim some imperative to serve their fellow human beings, though some are more emphatic about this conviction than others. I am well aware of the Christian ideal of service, which is viewed as a necessity of faith. However, I have been pleased to find others who do not share my faith but share my conviction of the necessity of serving others

While in India for special research, 1963-1964, I had occasion to help celebrate the centenary of the birth of the great Hindu leader of the Ramakrishna Mission and Math, Swami Vivekananda. In that connection I came across the following words of Vivekananda spoken to some of his disciples:

> I traveled all over India. But, alas, it was agony to me . . . to see with my own eyes the terrible poverty of the masses, and I could not restrain my tears. It is now my firm conviction that to preach religion to them, without first trying to remove their poverty and suffering, is futile. . . .[14]

I also recall an experience in India in which a Jain teacher became my friend and then introduced me to a wealthy Jain layman. This layman entertained the two of us at his home with a delicious vegetarian meal, the vegetables for the dinner having been grown on his own farm by methods consistent with the Jain conviction that there should be no injury to any animate being. At the teacher's suggestion, our host also showed us the school for poor children and the tuberculosis hospital that he had founded and financed and whose patients he regularly visited. In it all there was a noticeable air of humility about the man. I thought of Dorcas in the early church "who was always doing good and helping the poor" (Acts 9:36).

Of course, I do not mean to ignore the factor of motivation. Motivation to good works is very important, and motivations differ within as well as between religions. However, when a person is hungry, particularly a child, it makes little difference whether the bread given is Baptist or Buddhist, Muslim or Methodist. Surely there is a pressing need for cooperation between religions in meeting the tragic needs of suffering people.

<u>Getting at Root Causes.</u> Nevertheless, ministry to human needs, though very important, is not sufficient. There must be assaults upon the root causes of hunger, poverty and all that produces suffering. Why cannot religions unite in prophetic criticism of the evils that beset humanity and in social and political action to eliminate them? Religions should cooperate in opposing all tyrannies that deny human freedom and violate human dignity. They should denounce all present-day injustices such as racism and economic imperialism. The major religions, in varying degrees, have prophets and a tradition of strong prophetic criticism of the evils of society. Here, also, is an area for cooperation.

Violence of all kinds must be condemned. American society is marked by violence, and too many Christians participate in it, help to support it, or condone it. Other societies, likewise, are too given to violence. One particularly heinous kind of violence is terrorism. And we must not forget that certain types of fanatical, or not so fanatical, religion often foster or support terrorism.

One could speak, similarly, of the urgent need for religions to work together at the broader task of eradicating war and bringing a stable peace to the world. Think how many of the violent conflicts and civil wars in the contemporary world are in some profound sense related to religious quarrels. A primary challenge for religions today is to achieve peace among themselves. As Hans Küng has aptly said, "There will be no peace among the peoples of this world without peace among the world religions."[15] Religious relativism is not what Küng is advocating. Nor is it what I am promoting. Rather, the basis for interreligious cooperation is mutual respect among religions.

Then there is the task of saving the environment and all living creatures from pollution and destruction. Surely, here is a place where the various religions have their own ideas and teachings that could be joined with those of all people of good will to help with the solution of this most urgent problem.

And the list might be extended and the various items expanded upon. In any case, here is a large agenda for interreligious cooperation. It would be naive to expect that it will happen quickly or easily. Religions are often too aggressive, too coercive, too arrogant, and too prone to defend their own turf to join hastily in interreligious cooperation.

<u>Organization and Terminology.</u> Perhaps a good start would be the development of some all-embracing organization to effect such cooperation. The World Council of Churches may afford examples of the kind of structures needed, though I think it is confusing to use the terminology of Christian ecumenism for what we are discussing here. For example, among many others, Stanley J. Samartha, who has contributed so much to the development of good relations between religions, speaks of interreligious cooperation as the "larger ecumenism" or "wider ecumenism."[16] I think this use of terminology is a mistake. Of course, there is no problem concerning the meaning of the term *ecumenism*. Its usual meaning, based upon its Greek origin, is fostering the unity of that which is universal or worldwide, obviously applicable to the religions. Ordinarily, however, ecumenical terms have been used to express the cooperation and unity of different *Christian* groups, those who recognize that, in spite of their denominational differences, at a profound level they share a common faith. This usage of the term has a rela-

tively long history. To give it a broader meaning is to invite misunderstanding and fear of relativism.

Therefore, some new terminology is needed to describe this more recent kind of cooperation and proposals for cooperation that extend far beyond the Christian circle. *Interreligious* itself is not a bad term: interreligious cooperation, interreligious dialogue, interreligious unity. So long as it remains an adjective, it serves very well. It is unwieldy, but no more so, at least for some, than *ecumenical*. It is when a noun with similar meaning is called for that we have trouble. We need an "ism" to express in the interreligious context what *ecumenism* does in interchurch relationships. Maybe *interreligionism* will do, though it certainly is unwieldy, or *interfaithism*. Or do we need to create some other new word? Maybe, also, in the process of interreligious cooperation, dialogue will occur rather naturally. Deep matters of faith may be mutually shared most easily in situations where people of differing religions or ideologies are working shoulder to shoulder at the same task.

<u>Interreligious Worship</u> This last item of interreligious relationships, common worship, may well be the most difficult of all. To have dialogue in which sincere Christians tell what they believe and have experienced, while they listen carefully and respectfully to the testimony of others who do not share their faith is far less problematic than common worship. So is cooperation with religious believers who do not agree at all with the Christian faith. What matters is the common goal to serve others or to seek solutions for the world's pressing problems.

But how is common worship possible for people who do not agree at all on the nature of the Ultimate to whom prayer is addressed? How can you pray with folks who do not believe in any personal deity? Can we even say that the God of Christians is the same as the God of Jews or of Muslims? Philosophically, we believe that there is but one God, so of course the God of these three religious groups—not to mention other monotheists—is the same. Religiously, however, are the three actually the same? Jews believe in a God who specifically did not send Jesus as Messiah, at least to Jews. And Muslims believe in a God who specifically could not have Jesus as a Son.

The difficulty is well illustrated by an event that happened a few years ago, a conference of the day of prayer for peace, October 27, 1986, called by the Pope, and comprising fifty Christians and fifty invited representatives of other faiths. Although the gathering offered promise for the future, especially at the point of interreligious dialogue, it encountered some very thorny issues, the most nettlesome of which was the discovery that the participants, having been called to assemble for prayer, could not actually pray together. The various religious groups met separately for prayer. Not the least of the problems was that the Dalai Lama had been invited and accepted, though he had said earlier that prayer was unnecessary for Buddhists.[17]

Here, then, was a profound problem: people of the various religions felt that they could not conscientiously engage in common prayer. Is there any answer to this vexing problem? Maybe the Pope was getting close to the solution when he said, "Certainly we cannot 'pray together,' namely, to make a common prayer, but we can be present when others pray."[18] Frankly, I doubt the wisdom of calling people of different faiths together specifically for prayer. This puts too much focus on religious differences. It seems to me more fruitful to call an interreligious gathering for some other reason, have it understood in advance that one person, or several persons representing different faiths, will lead in worship, and then leave the matter of participation to individual consciences.

It is especially important that there be no hidden agendas but that everything be open and above board. If people are assured that interreligious worship involves profound mutual respect but not the lessening or compromising of religious commitments, then people may be able to participate in good conscience. *Spontaneous* prayer together is even better since it comes more naturally and involves some deep meeting of spirits beyond religious differences. Such is much more apt to happen with two persons or at most with a small group than with a larger assembly.

All this is to say that common worship is a very sensitive issue indeed, not possible in some circumstances, not impossible in others. It needs to be handled with great delicacy.

SPECIAL RELATIONSHIP TO CERTAIN RELIGIONS

Does the Christian religion have a special relationship to Judaism or to Islam or to all monotheistic religions?

Judaism: A Special Relationship and a Shameful History

Obviously, Christianity has a special relationship and an indissoluble link with Judaism as its mother faith. Even the Jewish Scriptures are accepted as the Old Testament or Old Covenant of the Christian Bible. Thus, Christianity is indebted to the Jews for that important part of her revelation that is the foundation of God's disclosure through Jesus of Nazareth. Christianity shares with the Jews the patriarchs and the prophets, and looks back to Abraham, the great ancestor of Israel, as the father of the faithful. Nor can the Church forget that Jesus himself was a Jew, nurtured in the faith of the Hebrew Scriptures, which we call the Old Testament. The apostles, also, who, with Jesus Christ as the chief cornerstone became the foundation of the Christian Church, were Jews. This inseparable bond of Christianity and the Jews is expressed by the Apostle Paul by the figure of an olive tree onto which the Gentiles have been grafted as wild branches (Romans 11:17-24). Likewise, Paul declared that to the Jews "belong the adoption, the glory, the covenants, the giving of the law, the worship, and the promises . . ." (Romans 9:4). Also, based upon the Pauline teaching, the Church awaits the day, known to God alone, when all peoples, including both Jews and Christians, will serve and worship God together.[19]

Unfortunately, in addition to this close relationship of Jews and Christians, there is also a long history of Christian persecution of Jews: forced conversions, accusations of deicide ("God-killing"), false rumors of Jewish atrocities, and anti-Semitism of frightful proportions. The worst of all was the Nazi Holocaust, in the perpetration of which, tragically, many Christians were involved, and many more were guilty of a silent sanction. All of this horrible history must be repented of and apologized for by Christians in the strongest of terms.

In the light of all this, to affirm a Christian witness to the Jew is problematic. Some Christians insist that our history has forfeited our right to such witness. Many believe that there is no Christian mission to the Jew. Surely it is a mistake for Christians to single Jews out for evangelism, as is sometimes done. Can it be that only a Jewish Christian, such as Paul and the other apostles, has a right to witness to a Jew?

I have often wished for a bridge community of Christians who retain much more of authentic Jewish culture in their congregational life than do Gentile Christians. Maybe our best hope for such Christians is in the Jews who believe in Jesus as Messiah and who worship in what they term "Messianic synagogues." Unfortunately, these Messianic Jews seem to be virulently hated and feared by the Jewish leadership. Insofar as I know about them, too many are very conservative in theology and aggressive in demeanor. Some, however, seem not only genuinely Jewish in culture but also Christian in spirit.[20]

Perhaps it should be pointed out that there are Jews who see a relation of equality and mutuality between Judaism and Christianity. Notable among these in recent history are the German philosopher Franz Rosenzweig (1886-1929) and the American sociologist of religion and theologian Will Herberg (1909-1977).

Though Herberg expounded and elaborated upon Rosenzweig's thought, their conclusions may be summarized as follows: Judaism and Christianity are necessary one to the other and will remain so until the end of history when adherents of both will be united as God's people. Judaism is the eternal light to which Christianity is the eternal way. Christianity is Judaism for the Gentiles. Gentiles must come to the Father through Jesus Christ, but Jews do not need to do so because they have always been with the Father. Jews see Jesus from behind, going out from them, while Gentiles see him from in front, coming towards them. Jews must *stand* faithful to God in an often hostile world, while Christians must *go* into that world. The Jew must always witness against the idolatries that beset Christianity because of its missionary encounter with the Gentiles, while Christianity must always witness against pride and exclusiveness and the over-emphasis upon chosenness in Judaism. Both are people of God with valid but different covenants.[21] This concept of two covenants is very attractive to many Christians, since some of its connotations are quite favorable to them.

Jürgen Moltmann recognizes his dependence upon Franz Rosenzweig without mentioning the two covenants. Nevertheless, he indicates that it is time to stress the convergences between Jews and Christians rather than their differences. He distinguishes between Jewish and gentile Christians and indicates that the first Christians became Christians not in spite of their Jewishness but because of it. "Therefore," he asks, "is not Jewish Christianity to be seen as a Jewish possibility? Is gentile Christianity not to be acknowledged as a Jewish-Christian insight and intention?"[22]

No doubt Christians will continue to differ among themselves concerning the responsibility to witness to Jews. In my judgment, Christians themselves must claim the right under God to interpret the Christian mission and not leave this important matter to people of other faiths, even our Jewish brothers and sisters. So far as we Gentile Christians are concerned, do we not have the privilege and responsibility for witnessing to the meaning of our faith without seeking conversions? I suggest that the Christian witness to the Jews must incorporate that profound sense of repentance I mentioned above. It must be a witness of genuine friendship, a friendship with no strings attached, a friendship that continues whether or not the Jew ever becomes a Christian. Probably in most cases it must be a silent witness, since Jews already know a great deal about us. We can never hope to have an effective witness to the Jews unless we *act like* the people committed to Jesus, the Messiah.

Many years ago, in a Christian-Jewish dialogue conference with the unfortunate theme of *conversion*—a term I have already suggested should be abandoned—as a member of a panel, I spoke in favor of the Christian witness to the Jew. My words drew harsh criticism from some Jewish scholars, including charges of bigotry and attempted genocide, but a rabbi came to my defense. "Copeland is right, you know," he said. "Copeland has to keep witnessing to me for the sake of his identity as a Christian. It is the nature of the Christian to witness. I must keep saying 'No' for the sake of my identity because I am a Jew."

Since the rabbi did not really know me, he probably did not know that my witness was usually silent and always, I hope, a non-threatening one. I profoundly appreciated and admired his statement. If I had been acquainted then with the insight of Jürgen Moltmann about the positive meaning of the Jewish "No," I might have adopted it as my own and mentioned it. Following Romans 9-11, Moltmann interpreted the salvation of Gentiles as wholly dependent upon the Jewish rejection of the Christian message. Gentile redemption is but a detour on the way to God's salvation of the Jews. Therefore, there is nothing more positive for the salvation of Gentiles than the Jewish "No." Conversely, there is nothing in the world more positive for the salvation of the Jews than the Christian faith of Gentiles,

> not so that Israel should accept the Christian faith and be able to enter into the Christian church. Precisely not that! But rather so that Israel might more passionately believe in *its* God and hope in *its* salvation the more it sees the faith of the gentile and the hope of Christendom.[23]

Islam: A Different Relationship with Similar Difficulties

What about the Muslim? Does Christianity have a special relation to Islam? In my judgment, yes, but of a very different sort from that of Christianity to Judaism. Islam shares with Judaism and Christianity respect for Abraham as its great ancestor, though Islam claims blood lineage with Abraham, not through his son Isaac, as do the Jews, but through his son Ishmael. Muslims, in the Qur'an, repeat some events of Biblical history and profess respect for certain of the prophets and apostles. Both Judaism and Islam are Semitic faiths, that is, deriving from those people known as Semites. Both are monotheistic, as is Christianity. Muslims, like Christians, are zealously missionary.

But there are profound differences. Islam arose several centuries after Christianity. Obviously, therefore, this religion, unlike Judaism, is in no way the foundation of Christianity. Rather, Islam claims to fulfill both Christianity and Judaism, since Muhammad is the seal of the prophets and the Qur'an is the final, infallible Scripture. Both Jesus and his mother Mary appear several times in the Qur'an, and in highly respectful terms. In the Qur'an, Jesus is represented as a prophet, and there are accounts of his virgin birth. He is given titles in the Qur'an, such as Messiah, which even Muhammad is not accorded. Muslims believe that they can correct the false picture of Jesus held by Christians, though the Qur'an repeats certain stories of infancy and childhood miracles of Jesus that Christians reject as a denial of the real humanity of Jesus and the reality of the incarnation of God in him. Likewise, the Qur'an teaches that Jesus was not really crucified; his enemies only thought they had killed him, but God took him up to himself (and therefore he was not resurrected).[24]

Some have even viewed Islam, at least before it became a separate and well-defined religious system, as an alternative form of Christianity. By the time Islam emerged, Christianity had become for the most part strongly Hellenized—especially taking on the characteristics of Greek thought. Hence there are those who think that Islam represented a new Semiticization of a Hellenized Christianity, and that both were probably heretical!

Muslims, like Jews, are strong monotheists. Even more emphatically than Jews, most of them believe that the doctrine of the Trinity is tritheism or polytheism. To believe in the Trinity is to be guilty of the heinous sin of *shirk*, the sin of associating something or somebody with God as sharing his deity. Unfortunately, it seems to me that Christians have too often given some basis for this charge of the abridgement of monotheism. We tend to grow up with a concept of three gods—God, Jesus and the Holy Spirit—or at least two—God and Jesus. And the language of "three persons" referring to the Trinity seems further to support this error, implying that God has three personalities. Whatever the meaning of the words translated from other languages into English as *person* (*hypostasis* in Greek and *persona* in Latin), in English the term connotes a separate personality. The Infinite may indeed transcend personality, but if personality is to be attributed to God at all, surely monotheism would require that God not have *three* personalities.

In any case, a discussion of the meaning of Jesus may well be the starting place for a dialogue with Muslims. However, it should be understood that Islam is very stony ground for the Christian mission. This is not only because of the Islamic conviction of an infallible revelation that has superseded that of Christianity. The difficulty is also exacerbated by an unfortunate history of relations between Muslims and Christians. Deeply etched in the Muslim's mind is the memory of the Crusades and the atrocities committed by Christians against Muslims (and others) in that unhappy era.

In addition, Christians are fearful of Muslim political dominance. Unlike Jesus, who deliberately refused political and military power as a means to religious ends, Muhammad accepted and employed such. As a result, Muslims usually cannot appreciate the separation of religion and politics that characterized Christianity in its pre-Constantinian history, and that, in differing measures, is true of areas today where Christians predominate. Nor do Christians relish the thought of being relegated to minorities in Muslim lands with only limited freedom and certainly without freedom to evangelize Muslims. The prospect of Christians living in countries ruled by Muslims, not to mention Muslim extremists, is not very inviting.

As a result, usually the Christian mission to Muslims is extremely difficult. In a way it is salutary that Islam stands as a stone wall resisting the Christian mission. All our great programs of "church growth," which seem to work so well in areas of Christian dominance or of primal religions, tend only to bloody themselves against the stone wall of Islam. We are thrown back upon the necessity of radical humility and the acceptance of the principles of incarnation and cross.

Other Monotheisms

As to the other religions, only three are clearly monotheistic. Zoroastrianism (Parseeism), was born about one thousand—some would say six hundred—years before Christ in ancient Persia. It is not of the Semitic branch of religions and is related to Christianity primarily through its influence upon early Judaism. Sikhism was founded about five centuries ago in India. Baha'i, the youngest of the world's living religions, emerged about a century and a half ago out of Shi'ite Islam, in

Iran. Though these three religions are not specially related to Christianity, each of the three has its own attractiveness and should be accorded respect from Christians. Baha'i, for example, strongly affirms modern progressive ideals.

* * * * *

But what is the nature of the redeemed community, and what is its future? If religions are to relate to each other as I have suggested, how are we to interpret their separate histories? What are the long-term results of these interreligious relationships? Is the ultimate future of the religions to be found beyond history? If so, what kind of future? These are the difficult questions the final chapter must address.

CHAPTER 6

The Redeemed Community, In History and Beyond

THE CHURCH

How are we to understand the nature of the church? Does the unprecedented meeting of Christianity and the other religions affect our perception of what the church is? If so, how?

Fellowship and Institution

I have already begged the question by using the term *the redeemed community* in the title of this chapter, have I not? Ideally, the church is the community of the redeemed. The Pauline metaphors of the church as the body of Christ or the bride of Christ are consistent only with the church as composed of the redeemed, the bride "without spot or wrinkle . . . holy and without blemish" (Ephesians 5:27). Since I do not know any church that fits this description, I assume that what is meant is the church in this ideal sense!

I take it that the city of God, the new Jerusalem, represented especially in the thought of Hebrews and Revelation, conveys the meaning of the church as ideal but also as eschatological. It is well to remember, nevertheless, that the redeemed universe, "new heavens and a new earth," comprises much more than the garden city (or church or redeemed community?)

that may well be at its center—however metaphorically this whole eschatological reality must be viewed. The new heavens and new earth represent a redeemed universe, not simply a saved community.

As ideal community, the church is the completely reconciled household of God. The divisions have been erased and there are no longer the determinative distinctions of race, culture, religion, social class, or gender, "for all . . . are one in Christ Jesus," as Paul puts it (Galatians 3:28).

The problem is that no such ideal church exists, though we may see hints of it here and there. The primitive church at Pentecost, described in Acts 2, may well be the model, or normative example, for this "Spiritual Community," as Paul Tillich suggested,[1] but even that church had to deal with such deceivers as Ananias and Sapphira, and it had not yet faced the problem of the Gentile inclusion. When it did, there were those who were Judaizers, who refused to accept the truth of the full universality of the church.

Obviously, the church is a fellowship, though in this life not an ideal one. But inevitably it is not only a fellowship but also an institution, at least in its pilgrimage through history. Even if, contrary to reality, the church as fellowship could escape defects in its life in this world, it could never merely be a fellowship. As soon as it effects organization of any kind, however primitive, it becomes an institution. And institutions are notoriously imperfect, not least because they always seem to become defensive and bent on their own self-preservation.

My own relationship to the church has always been a "love-hate" relationship, as we are wont to call such, though "hate" is far too strong a term to be appropriate in this context. I have been disillusioned and disappointed in the church many times, not least in the refusal of the church to face divisive issues but rather to wait until the secular society had first addressed these issues and had come to some decision about them. Tardily, then, the church has lined up behind secularists rather than led them, and this is an expression of a serious defect.

This fact of the church's spiritual tardiness was poignantly brought home to me several years ago, by correspondence from a woman with regard to what I had written in a church study course book about the ecumenical movement. This woman defended me—against very harsh critics—as having written objectively and not in a propagandizing manner, though obviously I had differed with the leadership of my denomination. She surprised me by stating that what I had objectively written could be discussed quite openly in the local John Birch Society to which she belonged but not in her local church!

However, I am a loyal churchman and I have often had to remind myself that the church is imperfect because its members, including me, are imperfect. Also, for all its failings, the existence of the church is fully justified if solely for the reason that it continues to preserve and transmit the gospel. No other institution could have been expected to do that.

"Anonymous Christians" and "Latent Church"

As institution, it is difficult for the church's leaders to recognize that it includes saved persons in other religious or nonreligious communities. An exception was the late Karl Rahner. In promoting an "open Catholicism," Rahner gave expression to the concept of "anonymous Christians." To be sure, there are those beyond the boundaries of the institutional or visible church who are among the saved, according to Rahner, but whenever they hear the gospel, these anonymous Christians become ecclesial Christians and part of the visible church. Thus in its institutional existence, the church is not to regard itself as the exclusive community of those who lay claim to salvation but as the vanguard of what it hopes is a hidden reality outside the visible church.[2]

Paul Tillich's concept of the "latent church" is similar but it has significant differences.[3] Tillich understood the "Spiritual Community," which is the church in its ideal sense, as present in manifold expressions in various religious and secular communities, for example, in Judaism, in other religions, and in secular humanism. Usually it is latent, but it may possibly be manifest. By "latent" Tillich did not mean merely potential; rather, he meant not yet manifest or adequately manifest—"partially actual, partly potential."

The Spiritual Community is latent *before* an encounter with the central revelation, which is the event of Jesus as the Christ, and manifest *after* such an encounter. It was through the death and resurrection of Jesus that the Spiritual Community became manifest within first century Judaism, and it is through the communication of that event that it becomes manifest since that time. Therefore, the Christ as Spiritual Presence and as Spiritual Community exists within the various religious and non-religious communities. Thus these communities are unconsciously drawn to the Christ, even if they reject him when he is presented to them through the missionary work of the churches. The fact that those outside the Christian community, whether in religious communities or not, are members of the latent Spiritual Community and not complete strangers is a powerful deterrent to Christian arrogance.

Both of these theological giants, then, Rahner and Tillich, were seeking ways to recognize that the church, as community, already existed beyond where its boundaries as institution extended.[4]

Church and Kingdom (God's New Order)

A similar motivation may have inspired Aloysius Pieris, a Sri Lankan Roman Catholic, to distinguish between the call to the kingdom of Christ and the call to membership in the church. Only the truly committed to the Christian teaching and way of life, a "little flock," were to be members of the church. However, the kingdom preached by Christ was already present among persons identified with the other religions. Christians thus could cooperate with members of other religions in order that the kingdom might further develop among them and the purposes of the kingdom and its justice might be advanced in their societies.[5]

It is likely that neither Rahner nor Tillich, in spite of good motivation, can escape the criticism that they were imposing a Christian identity upon persons who are not willing so to be labeled. Pieris does somewhat better, by carefully restricting the boundaries of the church in favor of the more universal dimensions of the kingdom, which I prefer to call God's new order.

At any rate, Pieris is not alone in distinguishing between church and kingdom. It is rather commonplace in Protestant theology to view the church as subordinate to the kingdom or as its servant. Official documents of the Roman Catholic Church have made this distinction only quite recently.[6] In my judgment, this distinction is quite valid. The church is not an end in itself. It exists to witness to the new order of God and to make concrete the ideals of this new order in history and in the universe which God has created. The dimensions of God's new order are always more expansive than are those of the church. Eschatologically, this new order may be understood as coextensive with the redeemed universe, while the church may be viewed as the redeemed human community within that much larger environment.

However, if the church is the redeemed community, that is, a human community on its way to a final redemption which is eschatological, then its boundaries cannot be confined to the visible or institutional church. I believe that we can admit the existence of those outside the institutional church, both in the religions and outside their memberships, who are nevertheless within the redeemed community and servants of the new order. And we can do so gladly and not grudgingly and without placing labels upon them, such as "anonymous Christians" or a "latent church." In an earlier discussion of salvation, I have already asserted my belief that there are saved persons beyond the Christian circle. To claim that the church as redeemed community extends beyond where it bears the Christian name is but to say the same thing in other words and in a different context.

In any case, there is absolutely no room for a sense of superiority on the part of Christians or of Christianity. Neither the Christian individual nor the Christian church has any monopoly on truth. As I shall emphasize later, there is no reason to believe that in the eschaton the redeemed community will be composed only of Christians or that the members of that community will even be called "Christians." The Christian ethic excludes arrogance.

SALVATION HISTORY

How should Christians understand the relation of salvation (sacred) history to other histories or world history? Is the salvation history to which the Bible testifies a universal history in which the various world cultures are to share? Are there several salvation histories corresponding to the various religious histories? Is there a *general* and a *special* salvation history paralleling general and special revelation? Is the history of God's action in Israel and the church the model by which we are to understand God's action in other histories?

Extra-Biblical Redemptive Events

The question of salvation history is a very difficult one. That there is within the Bible a salvation history (*Heilsgeschichte*) seems to be widely accepted by Christians. Just what it means, however, is quite another matter. For example, from the Christian standpoint, it is likely that there are saving events that have occurred after the production of the Bible was completed, though it would be hard to find agreement among Christians as to what these redemptive occurrences are. For example, is the Protestant Reformation an expression of salvation history? Or the emergence and burgeoning growth of Pentecostalism? If it is difficult for Christians to identify salvation history in the two millennia of the history of Christianity, surely it is all the more perplexing to affirm salvation history and to select saving events in other religions.

Redemptive History and "Chosenness"

Almost inevitably, at least for Jews and Christians, the concept of salvation history involves the sense of being chosen; both of these religions often see themselves as specially chosen of God. Stanley J. Samartha saw a polarity between the views of the priestly writers and the prophets of the Old Testament.[7] The former tended to view other nations from the standpoint of Yahweh's relation to Israel. The result was a sense of exclusiveness. Israel was viewed as the only chosen people of God.

The prophets, on the other hand, constantly challenged this assumption. They refused to see Israel only from the perspective of Mt. Zion. They demanded that Israel look at itself from the standpoint of the other nations. So Isaiah prophesied that "In that day Israel will be the third with Egypt and Assyria, a blessing in the midst of the earth, whom the Lord of hosts has blessed, saying, 'Blessed be Egypt my people, and Assyria the work of my hands, and Israel my heritage'" (Isaiah 19:24-25). And Amos declared: "Are you not like the Ethiopians to me, O people of Israel? says the Lord. Did I not bring up Israel from the land of Egypt, and the Philistines from Caphtor and the Arameans from Kir?" (Amos 9:7). Samartha remarked that it appears that other ancient peoples besides Israel had experienced exoduses just as there are many peoples today waiting to be liberated. Christians, wrote Samartha, have too easily sided with the priestly writers rather than the prophets, thus coming down on the side of exclusiveness.

I believe that Samartha has a valid point, though the prophets were by no means only seeking to draw Israel out of its national exclusiveness. Though not as consistently as the priestly writers, the prophets also sometimes gave expression to narrow nationalism and exclusivism. For example, Isaiah, after proclaiming oracles both against Israel and against the nations hostile toward her, then prophesied that the nations would restore Israel, but at the price of their own subservience. "The house of Israel will possess the nations as male and female slaves," wrote the prophet, and "will take captive those who were their captors, and rule over those who oppressed them" (Isaiah 14:1-2). And it would be difficult to find a more scathing denunciation of the idol worship of the nations than that of Deutero-Isaiah (Isaiah 44:9-20; see also 46:1-2, 5-7) or of Jeremiah (Jeremiah 10:1-16). Such distinctions between the religion of Israel and the religions of her neighbors—whatever their justification—tended to encourage exclusiveness.

Although in general I believe that Samartha was right, the question is whether we Christians are to understand peoples of other religions as having salvation histories, and if so how we are to understand them. A spirit of isolationism would argue for a salvation history confined to the Bible and those who accept it. I suppose it would be appropriate to ask adherents of other religions to answer this question for us. However, the concept of salvation history is a Christian idea, and it would seem unreasonable to expect people who are not Christians to apply to themselves a Christian notion.

Salvation History and World History

From the Christian standpoint, whatever salvation history there is in the Bible is set within the context of world history. Chosenness, or election, is strongly affirmed, but for the purpose of serving the mission of God.[8] But is sacred history to be confined to those who accept Biblical faith? If one believes that there is some revelation of God in the circle beyond where the Christian gospel is known, and particularly if one admits that this revelation has a salvific purpose, then surely there must be salvation history there as well, both in the history of culture in general and also in the history of religions.

Wilfred Cantwell Smith has argued persuasively for the unitary religious history of all humankind, "a history of religion in the singular,"[9] as he phrased it. For Smith, this one religious history in which all of us share is not a matter of debate; it is a fact, obvious to us once we see it. Not only so, "it is a matter of theological truth" as well.[10] Smith used several illustrations to support his claim for a universal religious history. In my judgment, his claim might have been strengthened by reference to the *axial* period of religious development, that remarkable millennium or so beginning about 1000 B.C.E when the major world religions had their origin,[11] and to the universal religious activity of the Middle Ages.

In any event, Smith's argument certainly shows that the histories of the several religions significantly overlap, and he may well be right in his contention for a unitary history of religion. The theological implication of his argument, of course, so far as salvation history is concerned, is that there is one salvation history in which all the religions share. This I am able to affirm, with the important proviso—unacceptable to Smith[12]—that the crucial event of the incarnation, death, and resurrection of Christ stands at the center of this salvation history as sole criterion for understanding its meaning.

Choan-Seng Song's view of the separate histories of the world's peoples as a continuation of creation is very appealing. He saw all histories as salvation histories in which Christ is present and active. He was especially impressed by the prologue to John's Gospel, in which creation and incarnation are united, thus setting history in the broader context of creation. Song believed that such an interpretation, rather than reducing the place of Jesus Christ in the Christian understanding of history and mission, would enhance it. That is, Christ would be freed from the bondage to *Heilsgeschichte* ("Redemption History") in which Western theologians had confined him, to be set in the larger context of history as the continuation of creation.[13]

In a later book, Song again affirmed his claim that salvation history could be found in cultures and religions outside Christianity. He called these phenomena "redemptive moments and redemptive events." He believed that "while fragmentary and imperfect," these evidences of salvation history were "nonetheless genuine," reflecting "in some way God's redeeming love and power that have become incarnate in Jesus Christ." Song related these salvific events to God's self-disclosure in creation throughout all history, which Paul recognized in the first chapter of his letter to the Romans. He identified some redemptive events in the history of Buddhism, particularly the self-immolation of Buddhist monks in Vietnam as a protest against the tragic and unjust Vietnam War and as a sacrifice for the sake of peace. The context of Song's discussion is the contrast of lotus and cross as symbols of Buddhism and Christianity respectively. He even called these two religions "comrades in arms" in the struggle for justice and peace in Asia.[14]

In the same book, Song expressed a remarkable sense of the eschatological meaning of history from the Christian viewpoint. He saw the resurrection of Christ as the clue to God's history, which begins where our human history ends:

> A new history begins each time the politics of the resurrection breaks into the life of people and into the history of nations. This history is new because it is open to the future. It is history created and sustained by the truth, freedom, and

love given to all humanity through the resurrection of Jesus Christ. It is a history of hope because it has been molded by the power of God's creating and redeeming love.[15]

Less appealing to me is H. R. Schlette's suggestion that there may be "general" and "special" redemption histories paralleling general and special revelation.[16] As I have indicated, I am not satisfied with the category of general revelation, since I believe that all revelation of God is through the eternal and cosmic Logos and that it is therefore always personal and not general. Since I reject the concept of general and special revelation, the idea of general and special salvation history related to this dual concept of revelation has little if any meaning for me.

I agree with Song that salvation history is present in the various separate histories of culture and religion. Indeed the implication of Song's view is very close to Smith's contention of a unitary religious history, in that Song understands these separate histories as grounded in the creation, which surely must give them some measure of unity. Song also believed that the redemptive events seen in the histories of the other religions, though "fragmentary and imperfect," are nevertheless genuine. I believe Song was right, though I am not quite so ready as he to identify this salvation history in the other religions. Also, I do not mind affirming as a matter of principle that the salvation history of the Bible, at the center of which is the determinative event of the incarnation, death and resurrection of Jesus Christ, is a model by which to understand God's action in other histories. It is the identification of the specifics that is difficult—probably not impossible, but difficult.

A TEMPORAL VISION

What is the Christian vision for the future of religions within human history? That Christianity will replace the other religions? That this displacement will be by means of fulfillment? That the religions will remain relatively unchanged? that they will reconceive their essences? that they will make their contribution to an emerging world faith? that the other religions will be transformed by the influence of Christianity without losing their identities? that Christianity will be enriched by its relations with the other religions to become more adequate as a world faith?

In an era of mass secularization, with religion no longer occupying the central place in human affairs in many cultures and with shrunken religious memberships in many places, it may be appropriate to ask whether religion *has* a future.

"The Future of An Illusion": Freud et al.

There are many persons today (some of whom may be in Christian churches!) who would answer this question in the negative, in spite of the growth and seeming popularity of religion. For countless people religion has become something foreign to daily experience. Apparently, they live day in and day out in a thoroughly secular pattern of life and give little or no thought to religion. It is a matter of so little interest to them that even the question of its future seems irrelevant. Some of their companions, however, see religion as positively harmful. They believe that religion is a drag upon human progress. To them, religion should have no future, and they hope that the human race will develop enough maturity to slough it off.

Although he has been dead for more than a half century, the great pioneer of psychiatry, Sigmund Freud (1856-1939), is a good representative of those who believe that religion has no future and deserves to disappear. In the latter period of his life, Freud turned to an interest in culture and its problems. He wrote two or three books in this area, among them a book on religion whose title, *The Future of an Illusion*, reveals Freud's attitude toward the subject.[17]

Freud believed that religious ideas were "illusions, fulfillments of the oldest, strongest and most urgent wishes of mankind." The terrifying experience of helplessness in childhood aroused the awareness of the need for protection, which was provided by the father. Then the recognition that this need continued beyond childhood made a heavenly father necessary.

It is often pointed out that Freud's orientation was to the religions of personal monotheism of the West, and that his interpretation of religion would be irrelevant to religions that did not believe in a heavenly father. While this criticism is generally valid, Freud had other ideas about religion that were more universal. He suggested that

> ... the benevolent rule of a divine Providence allays our fears of the dangers of life; the establishment of a moral world-order ensures the fulfillment of the demands of justice, which have so often remained unfulfilled in human civilization; and the prolongation of earthly existence in a future life provides the local and temporal framework in which these wish-fulfillments shall take place.[18]

In terming religion an illusion, Freud did not mean to say with certainty that religious doctrines were of necessity false. By illusion he meant a belief that had wish-fulfillment as a prominent factor in its motivation. At this point, although Freud sometimes accepted the designation *atheist* for himself, he actually seems to have been more of an agnostic. He recognized that an illusion, as he defined it, could turn out to be true. But he *believed* that religion was false and had no future. Why? Because, as he put it,

> ... in the long run nothing can withstand reason and experience, and the contradiction which religion offers to both is all too palpable. Even purified religious ideas cannot escape this fate, so long as they try to preserve anything of the consolation of religion. No doubt if they confine themselves to a belief in a higher spiritual being, whose qualities are indefinable and whose purposes cannot be discerned, they will be proof against the challenge of science; but then they will lose their hold on human interest.[19]

So all religious views, however lofty, would have to be abandoned. In this judgment and this prediction, Freud was speaking primarily as a scientist, not a psychoanalyst. So he ends his treatise with this statement: "... our science is no illusion. But an illusion it would be to suppose that what science cannot give us we can get elsewhere."[20]

Freud, then, is spokesman for scientifically oriented, secularized persons who have written off religion as an illusion that is either irrelevant or positively harmful, and, in any case, an illusion that should be outgrown. I remember an incident in Japan in the 1950s, in which a high school student told me, seemingly with some pride, that he had no religion. "I believe," said this student, "that all religion is superstition. As a scientifically oriented person, I cannot believe in religion." This viewpoint, though often less forthrightly expressed, was not at all unusual in Japanese educational circles. Though the growing rapprochement between religion and science may have rendered it less common, it is by no means rare even in the West. One evidence may be found in letters to the editor of various newspapers and news magazines.

"The Most Fundamental Element in Human Nature": *Toynbee et al.*

Over against the testimony of Freud one may set the witness of another noted scholar, Arnold J. Toynbee (1889-1975), the great historian or philosopher of cultures. Toynbee insisted that he had been an agnostic throughout his mature life. Though reared in an Anglican home, he could not accept the doctrines of Christianity and, indeed, could not feel at home in any of the world religions. Yet he had his own unorthodox religious faith, and he saw religion as important to the future of humanity.[21]

In an essay entitled "Encounters Between Civilizations," published in 1947, Toynbee made a striking set of predictions. He suggested that historians one hundred years hence, in 2047, will be saying that the greatest event of the twentieth century was the impact of Western civilization upon all other contemporary societies. After not another century but a millennium, in 3047, the historians will be impressed by the transformation of Western civilization by the influences from the East, from the Eastern Orthodox Churches, Hinduism and the ideologies of Eastern Asia. By 4047, a unitary world culture will have emerged, and historians will be able to see that the impact of Western civilization upon the East was the first step toward the unification of humankind in a single society. And, concluded Toynbee, in 5047, historians will be saying that the major factor in this unification of human culture "was not to be found in the field of technics and economics, and not in the field of war and politics, but in the field of religion."[22]

These predictions were made about fifty years ago when Toynbee was in his fifties. Fortunately, we have more recent statements from his pen against which to check his earlier appraisal of the significance of religion in the future life of the world.

In a partially autobiographical work published when Toynbee was eighty, he took pains to make clear his position on religion. Though he did not repeat his daring predictions of 1947, he reaffirmed his optimism concerning the future of religion. He stated his belief that religion is intrinsic to human beings, indeed "the most fundamental element in human nature." In his youth, he wrote, he had supposed that the historic religions were dying, and he had taken their imminent disappearance complacently. Now, however, he had seen them complete a cycle and re-emerge with new strength and promise. Toynbee indicated his belief, also, that in the twenty-first century, human life will be a unity in all its aspects including religion.[23] So he seems to have moved his timetable up considerably, from the fifty-first century to the twenty-first!

Obviously, then, honest students of human culture, scientifically oriented and intellectually brilliant, can read the religious evidence and project the future of religion in contradictory ways. This fact is but in keeping with religion, for religion by its very nature does not compel intellectual assent. In spite of its claims to truth, religion must remain a matter of faith.

The Question of Replacement and Fulfillment

However, if religion persists, as many of us, with Toynbee, believe will be the case, what will happen to the various religions? One possibility is that of replacement, that is, that Hinduism, for example, will be completely replaced by Christianity. This idea seems obviously imperialistic. Perhaps it should be buried along with the colonial past of which it was a part. The expectation of fulfillment is much more attractive, though it, too, is a kind of replacement and may be charged with imperialism. Fulfillment envisions that what is true and good, by Christian standards, will be embraced within Christianity so that the other religions no longer need to exist.

A problem with fulfillment is that the other religions have quite different points of departure from Christianity and therefore different quests. Christianity as a religion, and even the cosmic Christ *as Christians understand him*, may not be large enough to fulfill them.

The concept of Buddhist Christians, Hindu Christians, Confucian Christians, Islamic Christians and the like may be more realistic. Persons who have brought over certain elements of their own religious heritage into Christianity may feel that Christ has fulfilled their individual religious quests without necessarily assuming that Christ has fulfilled their religions as such.

Likewise, the idea that Christ may incarnate himself in another religion, Christ within Hinduism, Buddhism, Islam, and so forth, may be more realistic than fulfillment, though it is somewhat difficult to imagine what the consequences of such an incarnation may be. One meaning may be that some Christians will elect to remain within their own religious communities without baptism and membership in a Christian church. There are places where this is actually happening at present.

One World Faith and the Possibility of Reconception

In my judgment, one world faith is quite unlikely, however attractive may be its prospect. Human beings are too diverse for a unity at the point of their basic hopes and expectations. While we seem to be moving toward a world culture and an awareness of a world history in which we are all embraced, both a world culture and a world history will necessarily have within them a very wide diversity. Since variety seems to be a basic human quality, I suspect that the various religions will continue until the end of time, though some may cease to exist and others may be added, as, for example, Baha'i was added in the nineteenth century. But the religions will not continue unchanged. Each will be influenced by the others, and especially by the missionary faiths.

In this regard, the idea of *reconception* advanced by the late William Ernest Hocking, has some merit. My disagreement with Hocking is considerable. I do not agree with him in his seeming assumption that what was distinctive about Christianity was its teachings, even when these teachings are embodied in the founder of Christianity, Jesus Christ. Nor am I as sanguine as Hocking in his expectation that one world faith might emerge. Especially, I do not share his belief that the major religions had a common essence.[24] Nevertheless, Hocking's writings were impressive and his insights profound.

Particularly significant is Hocking's idea of *reconception*.[25] He rejects both *radical displacement* and *synthesis* in favor of *reconception* as the way faiths should relate to each other. Hocking carefully analyzed the advantages and disadvantages of radical displacement and found it unsatisfactory. By synthesis Hocking meant what we would usually refer to as *syncretism* in the negative sense. *Syncretism* is a perfectly respectable term which may be used positively for the process by which Christianity absorbed many alien elements in the course of its history. Nevertheless, Hocking regretfully rejected the term, precisely because of the extremely negative connotations that it conjures up. In the final analysis, Hocking refused the way of synthesis because it incorporated elements from other religions at the price of distortion of its true essence.

Rather, Hocking proposed "reconception" because it allowed the acceptance of elements from other religions without distortion. As such, he saw reconception as an acceptable variety of synthesis. In the light of the realities of other faiths, each religion must "reconceive" its own essence. Thus it should be able to indigenize without losing or perverting its own individual character.

Hocking saw reconception as a valid way toward a world faith, but he acknowledged that Christianity did not include all that other religions possessed and was not yet ready to assume the position of world faith. It is possible to accept Hocking's insight concerning reconception without sharing his qualified but rather optimistic expectation concerning a world faith. Surely vital religious faith can and will reconceive its essence in its confrontation with other religions. If the mutual relationship is positive, there is no reason why religions cannot mutually coexist, each giving its witness to the other, and each being influenced by the other. In my judgment, the Christian witness can be expressed quite validly in this kind of relationship.

TABLE ONE

Following are Hocking's own graphs illustrating what he meant by these three ways to a world faith: radical displacement, synthesis, and reconception:*

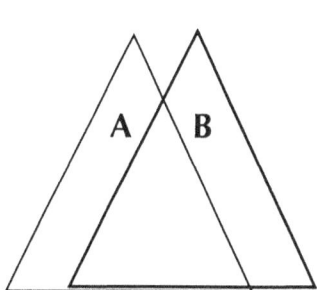

Two religions, A and B, are represented as being partly coincident or overlapping in their present teaching and character. The subsequent diagrams will represent the three ways to a world faith which we have now discussed, as practiced by A—religion B being assumed for simplicity's sake to remain passive.

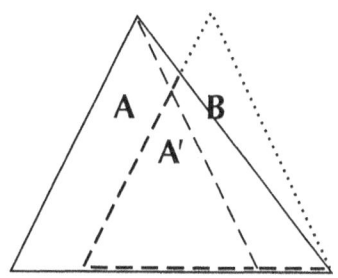

2. *Synthesis*
A reaches over to include what it finds valid in B, but with some distortion in its own shape.

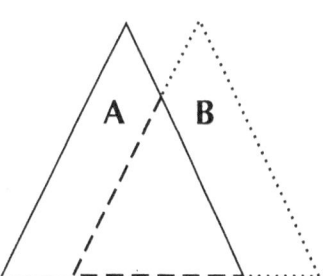

1. *Radical Displacement*
A hardens its own outline, excluding all of B except what is now included in A.

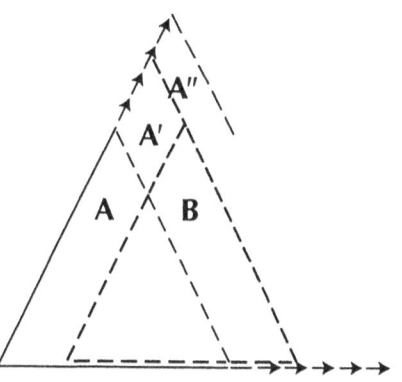

3. *Inclusion by Reconception*
The apex of the cone A, its conceived essence, moves upward, until without distortion the cone A includes what is valid of B, and indefintely more, as self-understanding deepens.

* William Ernest Hocking, *Living Religions and a World Faith* (London: George Allen & Unwin, 1940), 194-195

If Christian elements, and indeed if the Christ himself, should appear in other faiths, this is nothing to deplore but rather to applaud. Christians have neither the ability nor the monopolistic right to control how Christ may be interpreted by people of other faiths. It has already been noted that Christ has appeared in Hinduism and has exerted considerable influence within that faith. More and more we can expect this to happen. Somewhat similarly, the other religions may be expected to wield influence upon Christianity. It is important, however, that the process be reconception and not the kind of syncretism that distorts.

Co-existence with Mutual Influence

To sum up: of course, no one can predict the future with any measure of certainty. My own projection of the status of world religions in future history is extrapolated from what has happened thus far. Though unforeseen developments of the future may change the picture, there is no indication today that the prominent religions of Asia, notably Islam, Hinduism, and Buddhism, are on their way to extinction or that they will be replaced by Christianity, whether a reformed Christianity, changed by its relations with these religions, or a Christianity that remains relatively unchanged. Nor is there evidence of fulfillment of the other religions by Christianity—as distinguished from the fulfillment of the religious quests of individuals—which, as I have noted, is a form of replacement. The prospect for the foreseeable future seems to be that of co-existence with mutual influences.

This does not mean that the witness to Christ is to be muted. Quite the contrary. The message of Christ must be communicated in word, deed, and very life by those who are thoroughly committed to Jesus Christ and his mission. But what happens to the religions may well be left to God.

AN ESCHATOLOGICAL FULFILLMENT

But what of the future beyond history? May we look for an eschatological fulfillment in which only those confessing Jesus Christ as Lord will be the redeemed? in which each religion will find its own particular vision fulfilled—for example, Buddhists enjoying Nirvana while Christians engage in eternal fellowship with the God known in Christ? in which the metaphor of the City of God into which the nations have poured their cultural (and religious) riches will come to a new consummation embracing all earthly religions in some new and unforeseen completion?

The Eschatological Future and the Faith of a Christian

Obviously, the eschatological future can only be envisioned by faith. My faith is that of a Christian, and so also is my vision of the future beyond this life. Pluralism there may well be in the world to come, a pluralism that gathers up all the variety of the universe in new and unimaginable expressions. However, I cannot believe that in that eschatological city of God the particularities of religion will remain, so that Buddhists will enjoy Nirvana and other religions experience salvation precisely as their own teachings prescribe. If God is one, as Christians believe, surely there cannot be a situation wherein each human being, in isolation or in community, is worshipping her or his God or Absolute or whatever in segregation. Surely all will be worshipping the one God as one community, however difficult this may be to imagine. The Christian vision for the eschatological future—at least, *my* vision—is one of amazing variety in unity. All things will be reconciled to God through Jesus Christ and his cross, while all retain their individuality.

As I have noted previously, as a Christian I share with Paul the expectation that there will be a universal recognition of Jesus Christ as Lord as stated in Philippians 2:9-11. This means, I should think, that every distorted conception of God will be corrected, that we shall see God in all truth and reality, and Jesus Christ as one with God. Religious identities will no longer have any relevance. Titles such as *Christian* will not be used, I should think, as all will be gathered into one household of God.

The Eternal City of God

In that unimaginable consummation in the city of God, "the glory of God is its light," and "people will bring into it the glory and the honor of the nations" (Revelation 21:23, 26). The "glory of God," I assume, is the manifestation of God's mysterious and unique character which evokes awe, obeisance, and praise. "The glory and the honor of the nations" must surely be the notable achievements and unique characteristics of the various peoples of the earth—their cultures, including their religions—which will enrich the eternal city in some amazing and surprising completion.[26]

Actually, the city of God itself and all that characterizes it are couched in metaphorical language in the Bible, and it seems presumptuous to speak of this city at all—unless it is understood that what we say is also metaphorical. No doubt it is still true that "no eye has seen, nor the human heart conceived, what God has prepared for those who love him" (1 Corinthians 2:9), in spite of the fact that we are supposed to be able to speak of these matters "in words not taught by human wisdom but taught by the Spirit" (2:13). In any case, faith tells us that we and our universe, all of reality, God's total creation, are in for some indescribably wonderful transformation. It is pleasing to contemplate that we Christians have no corner on this amazing, renewed universe that is to come but will share it with all whom God loves and redeems, whatever names they may bear in history. If the universe as we know it, and the human community as we know it, are amazingly diverse, will not the redeemed universe preserve and fulfill all this remarkable plurality?

I remind you again that the above words are a testimony of faith, spoken by one who is a Christian. All that I have said is confessional, but I believe with all my heart that the gospel of Christ is true. Of course I may be dead wrong. All of us Christians may be wrong. Persons of some other faith may be right. Atheists may be right. Or, again, all of us may be wrong. At the very least, we enter into relations with adherents of other religions with what Monika Hellwig calls a "friendly wager." We bet our lives that the claims for Jesus Christ's unique and universal saviorhood and sovereignty are true.[27]

It behooves each of us Christians to be humble before mysteries that we do not understand. We have no right to claim as truth what God has not revealed to us. We walk by faith and not by sight. But persons of faith grasp their best visions of the future, commit themselves to them without reserve, and invest all their hopes in them. "For now we see in a mirror, dimly," and we "know only in part" (1 Corinthians 13:12), but "we do see Jesus" (Hebrews 2:9). And that is sufficient. As a Christian, with humble and joyous gratitude, I am committed to Jesus Christ. According to my own understanding, as God gives me grace and light, I must be true to him.

Conclusion

I BELIEVE THAT my own position has been expressed here and there in the discussion that has preceded. However, let me make it abundantly clear. As to the categories of theologies of religion that I have suggested in Chapter One, I am not persuaded by the usual pluralist arguments, attractive as I consider them to be. I am much closer to the nonrelativistic pluralism of Jacques Dupuis, though, as I have indicated, it is debatable whether this view should be called "pluralism." I respond most positively to the dialectical, confessional, and pre-eschatological agnostic categories I have indicated.

My view is dialectical in that I see all religions and their adherents as participating in the ambiguity of humanity. All of the major religions are products of revelation, on the one hand, and of human creativity and demonic influence, on the other. All of them and their followers sometimes respond positively and rightly to divine revelation, but sometimes wrongly and distortedly, at once seeking God and fleeing from God. All religions, including Christianity, may only be viewed ambiguously and dialectically. Christianity differs significantly only in that it gives witness, with however much perversion, to the central and crucial revelation of God in Jesus Christ.

My theology of religions is confessional. I believe that the communication of the Christian message should always be in the nature of testimony. My faith is no mere fideism. It is based upon what I believe is sufficient evidence, particularly the life, death, and resurrection of Jesus Christ and my experience of salvation through him. I also hold to the authority of the Bible as giving indispensable testimony to these revelatory and redemptive events. Although if I have the courage—which is by no means guaranteed—I am willing to die for my faith in Jesus Christ as universal Lord and Savior, I cannot claim any final certainty for this belief. Nor do I have the right to castigate those who apparently refuse the Christian gospel, since God is their only final judge. I do not know who is saved and who is lost. So I eschew a dividing of humanity into "we" and "they" categories.

I certainly believe that there is divine revelation in the whole of human culture, including the religions other than Christianity. Therefore, the revelation in Christ, though crucial and decisive, is not exhaustive, and Christian faith, in order to be complete, needs to be supplemented by the testimony of the other religions. I also believe that in this revelation God has a redemptive intent. Therefore, some, maybe many, who never hear the Christian gospel in this life will be saved, whether or not they profess the beliefs of a religion, but none is saved apart from the redemptive work of God in Jesus Christ. Perhaps it is also the case that some who hear the gospel and refuse it will be saved, since they reject the Christian message for valid ethical reasons.

Until the eschaton, we have no way of knowing who is saved and who is lost, who is right and who is wrong. As I perceive it, all our claims to truth and salvation, with whatever conviction we hold them, testify to them and live by them, have a certain tentativeness about them. They must wait upon the final denouement with Truth. This acknowledgment of tentativeness does not mean that we are left to flounder in uncertainty. Rather, it means that we have the certainty of a faith based upon what we perceive as sufficient reasons, not the certainty of laboratory experiment, and that we know the limits of our certainty and have the modesty and humility that those limits suggest.

Meantime, with this sort of attitude, as I have shown in Chapter Four, there is ample reason for us to go about the Christian mission to adherents of the other religions joyously, not as under some burdensome obligation but in fellowship with the One who has come to us in Jesus of Nazareth, and who is the motive and goal of our mission.

NOTES

CHAPTER 1: THE NEW ENCOUNTER AND THE CHRISTIAN THEOLOGY OF RELIGIONS

1. Leroy Rouner has made this point rather emphatically: Leroy Rouner, "Theology of Religions in Recent Protestant Theology," in *Christianity Among the Religions,* ed. Hans Küng and Jürgen Moltmann (Edinburgh: T & T Clark, 1986), 108. See also Richard Henry Drummond, *Toward a New Age in Christian Theology* (Maryknoll, NY: Orbis Books, 1985), xii.

2. Harold A. Netland, *Dissonant Voices: Religious Pluralism and the Question of Truth* (Grand Rapids, MI: William B. Eerdmans Publishing Company, 1991), 8.

3. E. Luther Copeland, *Christianity and World Religions* (Nashville: Convention Press, 1963). Revised edition published in Spanish: *El Christianismo y Otras Religiones* (El Paso, TX: Casa Bautista de Publicationes, 1977).

4. Alan Race, *Christians and Religious Pluralism: Patterns in the Christian Theology of Religions* (Maryknoll, NY: Orbis Books, 1982), 139.

5. Hendrik Kraemer, *The Christian Message in a Non-Christian World* (New York: Harper and Brothers, 1938), 112-113; and *Why Christianity of All Religions?* (Philadelphia: The Westminster Press, 1962), 88-89, for example.

6. Kraemer, *Why Christianity?* 104.

7. Lesslie Newbigin, *The Open Secret: Sketches for a Missionary Theology* (Grand Rapids, MI: William B. Eerdmans Publishing Company, 1978), 203.

8. Newbigin, *The Gospel in a Pluralist Society* (Grand Rapids, MI: William B. Eerdmans Publishing Company; Geneva: World Council of Churches Publications, 1989), 182-183. Emphasis mine.
9. The term "Third World" is at best ambiguous. If it means "developing nations," what about a country such as Japan? I am using the term because theologians of this area employ it.
10. See, for example, Rosemary Radford Reuther, "Feminism and Jewish-Christian Dialogue," and Marjorie Hewitt Suchocki, "In Search of Justice," in *The Myth of Christian Uniqueness: Toward a Pluralistic Theology of Religions,* ed. John Hick and Paul F. Knitter (Maryknoll, NY: Orbis Books, 1987), 137-148 and 149-161, respectively. See especially the essay by Suchocki.
11. Jon Sobrino, "Theology in a Suffering World: Theology as *Intellectus Amoris,*" in *Pluralism and Oppression: Theology in World Perspective,* ed. Paul F. Knitter (Lanham, MD: University Press of America, 1988), 153-154.
12. See Isador Imasogie, *Guidelines for Christian Theology in Africa* (Achimoto, Ghana: African Christian Press, 1983); Caritas McCarthy, "Christology from an African Perspective," in *Pluralism,* ed. Knitter, 29-47; Jackie Gene Partain, "Themes in Contemporary African Theology" (Ph.D. dissertation, Southwestern Baptist Theological Seminary, 1983).
13. See Wing-hung Lam, *Chinese Theology in Construction* (Pasadena, CA: William Carey Library, 1983), 79, and John 1:1, 14.
14. See Lynn de Silva, "Emergent Theology in the Context of Asia," in *Asian Christian Theology: Emerging Trends,* ed. Douglas L. Elwood (Philadelphia: The Westminster Press, 1980), 230.
15. See John Ross Carter, "Translational Theology: An Expression of Christian Faith in a Religiously Plural World," in *Christian Faith in a Religiously Plural World,* ed. Donald G. Dawe and John B. Carman (Maryknoll, NY: Orbis Books, 1980), especially 174-177.
16. An example is Raymond Panikkar, *The Unknown Christ of Hinduism* (London: Darton, Longman and Todd, 1964).
17. Caritas McCarthy, "Christology from an African Perspective." See also Jackie G. Partain, "Themes."
18. Virginia Fabella of the Philippines is a prominent editor of Third World women's theological writings. See, for example, *We Dare to Dream: Doing Theology as Asian Women,* ed. Virginia Fabella and Sun Ai Lee Park (Hong Kong and Manila: Asian Women's Resource Center for Culture and Theology and The EATWOT Women's Commission in Asia, 1989). See also the papers and re-

ports of the Second General Assembly of EATWOT (Ecumenical Association of Third World Theologians), Oxtepec, Mexico, 1986. These are published under the title, *Third World Theologies: Commonalities and Differences,* ed. K. C. Abraham (Maryknoll, NY: Orbis Books, 1990). About one-fifth of the contributors are women.

19. Choan-Seng Song, *Third-Eye Theology: Theology in Formation in Asian Settings* (Maryknoll, NY: Orbis Books, 1979), 10-11, 21.
20. Newbigin, *Pluralist Society,* 156.
21. See John Hick, *A Christian Theology of Religions: The Rainbow of Faiths* (Louisville, KY: Westminster/John Knox Press, 1995), 32-37.
22. Clark Pinnock, *A Wideness in God's Mercy: The Finality of Jesus Christ in a World of Religions* (Grand Rapids, MI: Zondervan Publishing House, 1992), 19.
23. Langdon Gilkey, "Plurality and Its Theological Implications," in *The Myth of Christian Uniqueness: Toward a Pluralistic Theology of Religions,* ed. John Hick and Paul F. Knitter (Maryknoll, NY: Orbis Books, 1987), 37-40.
24. Raimundo Panikkar, "The Jordan, the Tiber and the Ganges," in *The Myth of Christian Uniqueness: Toward a Pluralistic Theology of Religion,* ed. John Hick and Paul F. Knitter (Maryknoll, NY: Orbis Books, 1987), 109.
25. Ted Peters, *God as Trinity: Rationality and Temporality in the Divine Life* (Louisville, KY: Westminster/John Knox Press, 1993), esp. "Is the Trinity Interreligious?" 73-80.
26. For example, Kevin J. Vanhoozer, ed., *The Trinity in a Pluralistic Age* (Grand Rapids, MI: William B. Eerdmans Publishing Company, 1977).

CHAPTER 2: THEOLOGY OF RELIGIONS: REPRESENTATIVE VIEWPOINTS

1. Though there are many volumes that discuss this issue from the viewpoint of an individual theologian, there are others that are collections of essays by several scholars. Among these latter are two important books, one of which advocates pluralism and the other of which takes the opposite view. These are *The Myth of Christian Uniqueness: Towards a Pluralistic Theology of Religions,* edited by John Hick and Paul F. Knitter and published by Orbis Books in 1987; and *Christian Uniqueness Reconsidered: The Myth of a Pluralistic Theology of Religions,* edited by Gavin D'Costa and published by Orbis Books in 1990. The latter volume is a reaction or response to the former.

2. Many of Hick's voluminous writings set forth and defend his well-known pluralist position. See the extensive bibliography of Hick's works in Gavin D'Costa, *John Hick's Theology of Religions: A Critical Evaluation* (Lanham, MD: University Press of America, 1987), 215-231. See also Hick's own bibliography of his works on this subject and critical discussions of them in John Hick, *A Christian Theology of Religions: The Rainbow of Faiths* (Louisville, KY: Westminster/John Knox Press, 1995), Appendix II.
3. John Hick, "Whatever Path Men Choose Is Mine," in *Christianity and Other Religions,* ed. John Hick and Brian Hebblethwaite (Philadelphia: Fortress Press, 1980), 180-182. See also Hick, *Rainbow of Faiths,* 21.
4. Hick, *Rainbow of Faiths,* 44.
5. Hick, *Rainbow of Faiths,* 18.
6. Hick, "Whatever Path," 182-183. The term "Axial Period" is from Karl Jaspers, *The Origin and Goal of History,* tr. Michael Bullock (London: Routledge and Kegan Paul, 1953), chapter 1. The book was first published in German in 1949. Jaspers identifies the Axial period as about 800-200 B.C.E. Some would make its terminus a bit later to include Christianity.
7. Hick, "Whatever Path," 186.
8. Hick, "The Non-Absoluteness," 16.
9. Hick, *Rainbow of Faiths.*
10. Paul F. Knitter, "Catholic Theology of Religions at a Crossroads," in *Christianity Among the Religions,* ed. Hans Küng and Jürgen Moltmann (Edinburgh: T & T Clark, 1986), 103, 104. See also Paul F. Knitter, "Theocentric Christology," *Theology Today* 40:2 (July 1983), 134-137, 143-146.
11. Knitter, "Catholic Theology," 104, 106.
12. Paul F. Knitter, "Toward a Liberation Theology of Religions," in Hick and Knitter, eds., *The Myth,* 178, 181.
13. Knitter, "A Liberation Theology," 184, 194-195.
14. See, for example, his *Jesus and the Other Names: Christian Mission and Global Responsibility* (Maryknoll, NY: Orbis Books, 1996).
15. Knitter, *Jesus and the Other Names,* 18. I find it difficult to disagree with Knitter, partly because he is so sincere and honest, partly because he has so many good and true things to say about mission with which I am in agreement, and partly because his pilgrimage, in the course of which he has encountered the suffering other, the religious other, and the ecological other, is so reso-

nant of my own experience. However, I cannot identify with his pluralist position, and when Knitter writes honestly and fairly of his critics (*Jesus and the Other Names,* chapter 3), I find myself more convinced by his critics than by Knitter himself!

16. See especially Aloysius Pieris, *Love Meets Wisdom: A Christian Experience of Buddhism* (Maryknoll, NY: Orbis Books, 1988).

17. Aloysius Pieris, *An Asian Theology of Liberation* (Maryknoll, NY: Orbis Books, 1988), 59, 101-106.

18. Pieris, *Asian Theology,* chapter 8.

19. See Pieris, *Love Meets Wisdom,* 35.

20. Pieris, *Asian Theology,* 124.

21. Pieris, *Love Meets Wisdom,* 34.

22. Pieris, "The Buddha and the Christ: Mediators of Liberation," in *The Myth,* ed. Hick and Knitter, 162-177; see especially 171. This essay can be found, almost verbatim, in Pieris, *Love Meets Wisdom,* 124-135.

23. See Pieris, *Love Meets Wisdom,* 87-88.

24. Pieris, "The Buddha and the Christ," 175.

25. Pieris, "The Buddha and the Christ," 174-175. Another Christian theologian from Sri Lanka in some ways went beyond Pieris in his acceptance of Buddhist claims, namely, Lynn A. de Silva. See his *Reincarnation in Buddhist and Christian Thought* (Colombo: Christian Literature Society of Ceylon, 1968); and his *The Problem of the Self in Buddhism and Christianity* (Colombo: Study Centre for Religion and Society, 1975).

26. Raymond Panikkar, *The Unknown Christ of Hinduism* (London: Darton, Longman and Todd, 1964), 54.

27. Knitter, "Catholic Theology," 103-104.

28. Knitter, "Theocentric Christology," 136-137.

29. Also, his viewpoint is not free of contradictions. Tom F. Driver, in the same volume, points out that when Panikkar speaks of a "cosmic confidence" that "allows for a polar and tensile coexistence between ultimate human attitudes," he speaks of an impossibility. How, asks Driver, could an ultimate coexist, even with some tension, with other ultimates? Tom F. Driver, "The Case for Pluralism," in *The Myth,* ed. Hick and Knitter, 213.

30. Raimundo Panikkar, *The Trinity and the Religious Experience of Man: Icon—Person—Mystery* (Maryknoll, NY: Orbis Books; London: Darton Longman & Todd, 1973).

31. Raimundo Panikkar, "The Jordan, the Tiber, and the Ganges," in *The Myth,* ed. Hick and Knitter, 114.

32. Panikkar, "The Jordan," 110.
33. Panikkar, "The Jordan," 113-114.
34. In Panikkar, "The Jordan," 109; and Panikkar, "Can Theology Be Transcultural?" in *Pluralism and Oppression: Theology in World Perspective,* ed. Paul Knitter (Lanham, MD: University Press of America, 1991), 14. In the latter reference, Panikkar wrote: "Neither exclusivism nor inclusivism is any longer convincing. Pluralism is the name of our third position."
35. Rowan Williams, "Trinity and Pluralism," in *Christian Uniqueness Reconsidered: The Myth of a Pluralistic Theology of Religions,* ed. Gavin D'Costa (Maryknoll, NY: Orbis Books, 1990), 6.
36. See Panikkar, "Can Theology Be Transcultural?," 11-18, for instance.
37. Panikkar, "The Jordan," 184.
38. Stanley J. Samartha, "The Cross and the Rainbow: Christ in a Multireligious Culture," in *Christian Uniqueness Reconsidered,* ed. Hick and Knitter, 69-88.
39. See, for example, his statement concerning the significance of Christ for "all cultures and all ages," in Samartha, "Dialogue as a Continuing Christian Concern," in *Living Faiths and the Ecumenical Movement,* ed. S. J. Samartha (Geneva: World Council of Churches, 1971), 154-155.
40. Samartha, "The Cross and the Rainbow," 70, 83, 79-81.
41. Samartha, *One Christ–Many Religions: Toward a Revised Christology* (Maryknoll, NY: Orbis Books, 1991). See especially chapters 9 and 10.
42. *One Christ–Many Religions,* 137.
43. *One Christ–Many Religions,* 122.
44. *One Christ–Many Religions,* 83, 124.
45. *One Christ–Many Religions,* 116.
46. *One Christ–Many Religions,* 153-154.
47. Jacques Dupuis, *Toward a Christian Theology of Religious Pluralism* (Maryknoll, NY: Orbis Books, 1997).
48. Dupuis, *Religious Pluralism,* chapters 5-6.
49. Dupuis, *Religious Pluralism,* 11, for example.
50. Dupuis, *Religious Pluralism,* 13-19.
51. See the useful summary on 305.
52. Dupuis, *Religious Pluralism,* 282.
53. Dupuis, *Religious Pluralism,* 319-321.

54. Dupuis, *Religious Pluralism,* 326.
55. Dupuis, *Religious Pluralism,* 268-279, esp. 274-279.
56. Dupuis, *Religious Pluralism,* 386-390.
57. Dupuis, *Religious Pluralism,* 326-329.
58. Dupuis, *Religious Pluralism,* 284, 209, n.11.
59. Dupuis, *Religious Pluralism,* 328-329.
60. These books are *John Hick's Theology of Religions: A Critical Evaluation* (Lanham, MD: University Press of America, 1987) and *Theology and Religious Pluralism* (Oxford: Basil Blackwell, 1986).
61. Gavin D'Costa, "Christ, the Trinity and Religious Plurality," in *Christian Uniqueness Reconsidered: The Myth of a Pluralistic Theology of Religions,* ed. Gavin D'Costa (Maryknoll, NY: Orbis Books, 1990), 18. Emphasis in original.
62. D'Costa, "Trinity," 22-23.
63. I repeat that my term for kingdom is *God's new order*.
64. D'Costa, "Trinity," 19-22.
65. D'Costa, "Trinity," 23-26.
66. Georges Khodr, "The Economy of the Holy Spirit," in *Mission Trends No. 5, Faith Meets Faith,* ed. Gerald H. Anderson and Thomas F. Stransky (New York: Paulist Press, and Grand Rapids, MI: William B. Eerdmans Publishing Company, 1981), 37-40. This article was first published in the *Ecumenical Review,* April 1971.
67. Khodr, "The Economy," 46-47.
68. Georges Khodr, "An Orthodox Perspective on Inter-Religious Dialogue," *Current Dialogue, 19* (January 1991), 25-27. (This article first appeared in World Council of Churches, *Dialogue with People of Living Faiths,* 1981).
69. Here Khodr was referring to the traditional understanding of the Trinity as three *hypostases,* often translated into English—incorrectly, in my judgment—as three *persons*. A "monohypostatic" view of God would be a blurring of any distinctions in the Godhead.
70. Khodr, "Orthodox Perspective," 25-27. (It is interesting that in this article Khodr affirmed the *filioque,* that is, that the Holy Spirit proceeds from the Father *and the Son,* a position the Orthodox Church has traditionally refused and the Western Churches—Roman Catholic and Protestant—have affirmed. Wrote Khodr: "The Son is understood in His eternal reciprocity with the Spirit, receiving it and *sending* it into the world," 25. Emphasis mine.)

71. Khodr, "Orthodox Perspective," 27.
72. Khodr, "Orthodox Perspective," 26.
73. Khodr, "Orthodox Perspective," 27.
74. Kenneth Cragg, *Christ and the Faiths* (Philadelphia: The Westminster Press, 1986).
75. Cragg, *Christ and the Faiths,* 263.
76. See especially Cragg, *Christ and the Faiths,* 22-23, 329-334.
77. Norman Anderson, *Christianity and World Religions, The Challenge of Pluralism* (Downer's Grove, IL: Inter-Varsity Press, 1984), 143-155. (This is an enlarged and updated version of a 1970 edition with the title, *Christianity and Comparative Religion.*)
78. Anderson, *Christianity and World Religions,* 172.
79. Anderson, *Christianity and World Religions,* 172-174.
80. John B. Cobb, Jr., *Beyond Dialogue* (Philadelphia: Fortress Press, 1982), 85. Cited by Rouner, "Theology of Religions," 115.
81. John B. Cobb, Jr., *Christ in a Pluralistic Age* (Philadelphia: The Westminster Press, 1975), 21-22, 24.
82. John B. Cobb, Jr., "Beyond Pluralism," in *Uniqueness,* ed. D'Costa, 81-95.
83. Cobb, "Beyond Pluralism," 92-94.
84. Lesslie Newbigin, *The Finality of Christ* (London: SCM Press, 1969).
85. Lesslie Newbigin, *The Open Secret: Sketches for a Missionary Theology* (Grand Rapids, MI: William B. Eerdmans Publishing Company, 1978), 181.
86. Lesslie Newbigin, *Trinitarian Faith and Today's Mission* (Richmond, VA: John Knox Press, 1964), especially chapter 4. First published by Edinburgh House Press, 1963.
87. Newbigin, *The Open Secret,* 184-191. In a later essay, Newbigin again trenchantly criticized Hick and other pluralists who had published essays in *The Myth,* ed. Hick and Knitter. Newbigin, "Religion for the Marketplace," in *Christian Uniqueness,* ed. D'Costa, 135-148.
88. Newbigin, *Secret,* 191-197.
89. Newbigin, *Secret,* 197-205.
90. Walter Freytag, *The Gospel and the Religions* (London: SCM Press, 1957), 21.
91. From this point, Newbigin briefly but insightfully discussed interreligious dialogue.

92. Newbigin, *The Gospel in a Pluralist Society*, 155-170.
93. Newbigin, *The Gospel in a Pluralist Society*, 176-183.
94. Ajith Fernando, *The Christian's Attitude Toward Other Religions* (Wheaton, IL: Tyndale House Publishers, 1987), 47, 91- 103.
95. Fernando, *The Christian's Attitude*, 92-113.
96. Fernando, *The Christian's Attitude*, 52.
97. Fernando, *The Christian's Attitude*, 113-114, 119.
98. Fernando, *The Christian's Attitude*, chapters 9 and 10.
99. Fernando, *The Christian's Attitude*, 144-146.
100. Clark Pinnock, *A Wideness in God's Mercy: The Finality of Jesus Christ in a World of Religions* (Grand Rapids, MI: Zondervan Publishing House, 1992), 15.
101. Pinnock, *A Wideness*, chapter 1.
102. Pinnock, *A Wideness*, chapter 2.
103. Pinnock, *A Wideness,*, 14.
104. Pinnock, *A Wideness*, chapters 3 and 4, especially 146-147.
105. Pinnock, *A Wideness*, 178. See all of chapter 5.

CHAPTER 3: ARTICULATING THE QUESTIONS

1. See Kraemer, *Religion and the Christian Faith* (London: Lutterworth Press, 1956), 58-63, and *The Christian Message*, 102.
2. Knitter, "A Liberation Theology," 183-184. Gilkey, "Plurality," 49.
3. All Bible quotations are from *The New Standard Revised Version* (Nashville, TN: Thomas Nelson Publishers, 1989).
4. D'Costa, "Christ, the Trinity," 19-26; John V. Taylor, *The Go-Between God: The Holy Spirit and the Christian Mission* (Philadelphia: Fortress Press, 1973); and D'Costa, "Christ, the Trinity," 16-29.
5. *The First Apology of Justin,* chapter 46, in *Ante-Nicene Fathers,* vol. 1 (Grand Rapids, MI: William B. Eerdmans Publishing Company, 1953), 178.
6. *The Second Apology of Justin,* chapter 10, in *Ante-Nicene Fathers,* vol. 1, 191.
7. A. C. Bouquet, "Revelation and the Divine Logos," in *The Theology of the Christian Mission,* ed. Gerald H. Anderson (New York: McGraw-Hill Book Company, 1961), 192-194.
8. Paul Tillich, *Dynamics of Faith* (New York: Harper and Brothers, 1957), 45. Cited in Choan-Seng Song, *Third-Eye Theology: Theology in Formation in Asian Settings* (Maryknoll, NY: Orbis Books, 1979), 114.

9. Gilkey, "Plurality," 44.
10. Newbigin, *Secret,* 191-205.
11. Anderson, *Christianity and World Religions,* 172.
12. Hendrik Kraemer, "Continuity or Discontinuity," in International Missionary Council, *The Authority of the Faith, Madras Series,* Volume I (New York: International Missionary Council, 1939), 1- 21.
13. In Kraemer, *Religion and the Christian Faith,* 231-233, and in Kraemer, *Why Christianity of All Religions?,* 96. These books were published in 1956 and 1962, respectively.
14. Kraemer, *Religion and the Christian Faith,* 332-333, for example.
15. Don Richardson, *Eternity in Their Hearts,* revised edition (Ventura, CA: Regal Books, 1981), 117-122.
16. Frederick Faber's Hymn, "There's a Wideness in God's Mercy," *The New Church Hymnal,* ed. H. Augustine Smith et al. (New York: Fleming H. Revell Company, 1937), Hymn No. 82.
17. I have always suspected that Balaam got a bad rap in the New Testament (2 Peter 2:15-16; Jude 11; Revelation 2:14). Balaam was greedy, but he resisted his own greediness and obeyed God, albeit reluctantly, according to the story in Numbers 22-24. Balak, king of Moab, seems to have been the real culprit. Other places in the Old Testament are considerably more negative about Balaam, however (Numbers 31:8,16; Deuteronomy 23:4; Joshua 13:22, 24:9-10; and Nehemiah 13:2). Perhaps they influenced the New Testament view. Some would see the speech of the donkey as an example of divine inspiration by dictation!
18. Harold Lindsell, *An Evangelical Theology of Missions* (Grand Rapids, MI: Zondervan Publishing House, 1970). This book is a republication of a volume published much earlier, entitled *A Christian Philosophy of Missions* (Wheaton, IL: Van Kampen, 1949).
19. Richardson, *Eternity;* and Fernando, *The Christian's Attitude.*
20. Emil Brunner, *Revelation and Reason: The Christian Doctrine of Faith and Knowledge,* tr. Olive Wyon (Philadelphia: Westminster Press, 1946), 63-66.
21. See, for example, J. Herbert Kane, *Understanding Christian Missions* (Grand Rapids, MI: Baker Book House, 1974), 127-137; and Millard J. Erickson, "Hope for Those Who Haven't Heard? Yes, But . . . ," *Evangelical Missions Quarterly,* 11:2 (April 1975), 122-126.
22. Pinnock, *A Wideness,* chaps. 2 and 5.
23. Paul Tillich, *Systematic Theology,* vol. I (Chicago: The University of Chicago Press, 1951), 283-285.

24. William Ernest Hocking, *Living Religions and a World Faith* (London: George Allen & Unwin, 1940), 170.
25. Netland, *Dissonant Voices,* 276, n. 106.
26. On the other side of this issue, see the exegesis in Fernando, *The Christian Attitude,* 140-144.
27. C. R. North, "Sacrifice," in *A Theological Wordbook of the Bible,* ed. Alan Richardson (New York: The Macmillan Company, 1950), 206.
28. Alfred Lord Tennyson, "In Memoriam," *Tennyson's In Memoriam,* ed. William J. Rolfe (Boston: Houghton Mifflin & Company, 1895), LIV, 60.

CHAPTER 4: THE CHRISTIAN MISSION AND OTHER MISSIONS

1. Knitter, *Jesus and the Other Names,* 57 and chapter 7.
2. E. Luther Copeland, *World Mission and World Survival: The Challenge and Urgency of Global Missions Today* (Nashville, TN: Broadman Press, 1985), 136-137.
3. James S. Stewart, *Thine Is the Kingdom* (New York: Charles Scribner's Sons, 1956), 7.
4. Wilfred Cantwell Smith, *Towards a World Theology: Faith and the Comparative History of Religion* (Philadelphia: The Westminster Press, 1981), 168-171.
5. Copeland, *Mission and Survival,* 139-141.
6. Kosuke Koyama, "What Makes a Missionary? Toward Crucified Mind Not Crusading Mind," in *Mission Trends No. 1,* ed. Gerald Anderson and Thomas Stransky (New York: Paulist Press and Grand Rapids, MI: William B. Eerdmans Publishing Company, 1974), 130-132.
7. Copeland, *Mission and Survival,* 109.
8. John A. Mackay, *Ecumenics,* (Englewood Cliffs, NJ: Prentice Hall, 1964), 178-179.
9. Kraemer, *The Christian Message,* 140. [Note the sexist language, characteristic of Kraemer's day.]
10. Knitter, *Jesus and the Other Names,* 142.
11. The term "purpose" is used in Donald A. McGavran, *Understanding Church Growth* (Grand Rapids, MI: William B. Eerdmans Publishing Company, 1970), 32.
12. Donald A. McGavran, *Momentous Decisions in Missions Today* (Grand Rapids, MI: Baker Book House, 1984), 100, 168-178; and *Understanding Church Growth,* 32, 198.
13. McGavran, *Understanding Church Growth,* 35-36.

14. McGavran, *Momentous Decisions*, 64-66.
15. Choan-Seng Song, *Christian Mission in Reconstruction—An Asian Analysis* (Maryknoll, NY: Orbis Books, 1977), 268.
16. See, for example, *World Christian Encyclopedia*, edited by David Barrett (New York: Oxford University Press, 1982), 19.
17. Jürgen Moltmann, "Christianity and the World Religions," in *Christianity and the Other Religions*, ed. John Hick and Brian Hebblethwaite (Philadelphia: Fortress Press, 1980), 193-194. The term "critical catalyst" is Hans Küng's.
18. Wilfred Cantwell Smith, "Participation: The Changing Christian Role in Other Cultures," in *Religious Diversity: Essays of W. C. Smith*, ed. Willard T. Oxtoby (New York: Harper and Row, 1976), chapter 7, especially 129-132.
19. Copeland, *Mission and Survival*, 122-123.
20. Wilfred Cantwell Smith, "The Future of the Church and the Future of Mission," in *The Church in the Modern World*, ed. George Johnston and Wolfgang Roth (Toronto, ON: The Ryerson Press, 1967), 166-167.
21. Samartha, *Courage for Dialogue*, 101.
22. Compare Gilkey, "Plurality," 45.

CHAPTER 5: INTERRELIGIOUS RELATIONSHIPS

1. Hendrik Kraemer, *World Cultures and World Religions: The Coming Dialogue* (Philadelphia: The Westminster Press, 1960), esp. 15. Emphasis mine.
2. Reuel L. Howe, *The Miracle of Dialogue* (New York: Seabury Press, 1963), 37.
3. It does not help that many people seem to think that *dialogue* is somehow limited to two: two persons, two groups, two religions. But, of course, *dia* means *through*. Etymologically, *dialogue* has no numerical limitation and can include any number of persons or parties. Some scholars, however, have invented the word *trialogue* to mean conversations between three parties.

    For those who are not convinced that *dialogue* is adequate, there is W. C. Smith's helpful suggestion of *colloquy* as a better term; *World Theology*, 193.
4. Paul Knitter, for example. See his *Jesus and the Other Names*, esp. chapter 2.
5. M. A. C. Warren, "General Introduction," in John V. Taylor, *The Primal Vision* (Philadelphia: Fortress Press, 1963), 10.

6. Paul Tillich, *Christianity and the Encounter of the World Religions* (New York: Columbia University Press, 1963), 62.
7. Lesslie Newbigin, "The Basis, Purpose and Manner of Inter-Faith Dialogue," in *Interreligious Dialogue: Facing the Next Frontier,* vol. 1, ed. Richard W. Rousseau (Scranton, PA: Ridge Row Press, 1981), 25.
8. Newbigin, "Interfaith Dialogue," 28.
9. Newbigin, "Interfaith Dialogue," 25.
10. John V. Taylor, "The Theological Basis of Interfaith Dialogue," in *Christianity and Other Religions,* ed. Hick and Hebblethwaite, 221-227.
11. Newbigin, *The Gospel in a Pluralist Society,* 182.
12. World Council of Churches, *Guidelines on Dialogue with People of Living Faiths and Ideologies* (Geneva: World Council of Churches, 1979), 14-15.
13. Choan-Seng Song, *Third-Eye Theology: Theology in Formation in Asian Settings* (Maryknoll, NY: Orbis Books, 1979), 119.
14. *Swami Vivekananda Centenary Memorial Volume,* ed. R. C. Majumdar (Calcutta: Swami Vivekananda Centenary, 1963), 162.
15. Hans Küng, *Christianity and the World Religions* (Garden City, NY: Doubleday and Company, 1986), 443.
16. S. J. Samartha, *Courage for Dialogue: Ecumenical Issues in Inter-Religious Relationships* (Geneva: World Council of Churches, 1981), 43, 44. The very title applies ecumenical terminology to interreligious relationships.
17. See the description of this meeting and its difficulties in Samartha, *One Christ,* 14-16.
18. Samartha, *One Christ,* 16.
19. See "Declaration on the Relationship of the Church to Non Christian Religions," in *The Documents of Vatican II,* ed. Walter M. Abbott and Joseph Gallagher (New York: Guild Press, America Press, Association Press, 1966), 663-667.
20. See, for example, Fana Spielburg and Stuart Daumermann, "Contextualization: Witness and Reflection, Messianic Jews as a Case," *Missiology,* 25(1): 15-35.
21. See the excellent discussion of these two Jewish thinkers in Edmund Perry, *The Gospel in Dispute: The Relation of Christian Faith to Other Missionary Religions* (Garden City, NY: Doubleday & Company, 1958), 123-131.
22. Pinchas Lapide and Jürgen Moltmann, *Jewish Monotheism and Christian Trinitarian Thought* (Philadelphia: Fortress Press, 1981), 55-56.

23. *Ibid.,* 89-90.
24. There are many English translations (or interpretations) of the Qur'an. Usually, an index to the translation will indicate the teachings about Christianity that I have suggested.

CHAPTER 6: THE REDEEMED COMMUNITY IN HISTORY AND BEYOND

1. Paul Tillich, *Systematic Theology,* vol. 3 (Chicago: University of Chicago Press, 1963), 149-161.
2. Karl Rahner, "Christianity and the Non-Christian Religions," in *Christianity and the Other Religions,* ed. Hick and Hebblethwaite, 52-79.
3. See *Systematic Theology,* vol. 3, esp. 152-155.
4. It has always seemed to me remarkable that Rahner, the Catholic, wrote about individual Christians, while Tillich, the Protestant, focused upon the church. Since Catholicism is supposed to be collective and Protestantism individualistic, the opposite might have been expected.
5. Pieris, *Love Meets Wisdom,* 34.
6. These documents are the papal encyclical *Redemptoris Missio* and the Vatican treatise *Dialogue and Proclamation.* See extensive excerpts from the former in *International Bulletin of Missionary Research* 15 (April 1991): 50-52; and in *New Directions in Mission and Evangelization 1: Basic Statements, 1974-1991,* ed. James A. Scherer and Stephen B. Bevans (Maryknoll, NY: Orbis Books, 1992), 169-176. For the latter, see *Bulletin of the Pontifical Council on Interreligious Dialogue* 26:2 (Rome: Vatican Polyglot Press, 1991); and the discussion in Knitter, *Jesus and the Other Names,* 118-119, 125-139.
7. Samartha, *Courage for Dialogue,* 99-100.
8. See H. H. Rowley, *The Biblical Doctrine of Election* (London: Lutterworth Press, 1950).
9. Smith, *World Theology,* title of chapter 1.
10. Smith, *World Theology,* 3-4.
11. See Jaspers, *Origin and Goal,* chapter 1.
12. I do not agree with Smith's theocentric pluralism (although he appeals to Christ as criterion for understanding God's revelation in the world of religions—see *World Theology,* 170-171, for example), but I find that he has much to say that is instructive and provocative.
13. Song, *Christian Mission,* chapter 2, esp. 30-35.

14. Song, *Third-Eye Theology,* 115-123.
15. Song, *Third-Eye Theology,* 259.
16. Heinz Robert Schlette, *Towards a Theology of Religions* (New York: Herder and Herder, 1966), especially Part 3.
17. Sigmund Freud, *The Future of an Illusion,* revised Anchor Books edition, edited and translated by W. D. Robson-Scott (Garden City, NY: Doubleday and Company, 1964). This little book was first published in German in 1927. The relation of Freud's view to that of Ludwig Feuerbach (1809-1872), who influenced not only Freud's but also Karl Marx's interpretation of religion, is obvious.
18. Freud, *Illusion,* 47-48.
19. Freud, *Illusion,* 89.
20. Freud, *Illusion,* 92.
21. Arnold Toynbee, *Experiences* (New York: Oxford University Press, 1969), 125ff.
22. Toynbee, "Encounters Between Civilizations," *Civilization on Trial* (New York: Oxford University Press, 1969), 213-224. This essay was first published in *Harper's Magazine,* April, 1947. The quotation is from p. 216.
23. Toynbee, *Experiences,* 110, 146, 216, 321-322.
24. For his view on the idea of a common essence, see especially William Ernest Hocking, *The Coming World Civilization* (New York: Harper and Brothers, 1956), 145-150. See also Commission of Appraisal, William Ernest Hocking, Chairman, *Re-Thinking Missions: A Laymen's Inquiry after One Hundred Years* (New York: Harper and Brothers, 1932), 37.
25. See Table One and Hocking, *Living Religions and a World Faith* (London: George Allen & Unwin, 1940), 143-208, 249-262.
26. Copeland, *World Mission,* 143.
27. Monika Hellwig, "Christology in the Wider Ecumenism," in *Christian Uniqueness Reconsidered,* ed. Gavin D'Costa, 111.

BIBLIOGRAPHY

Abbott, Walter M., and Joseph Gallagher. *The Documents of Vatican II.* New York: Guild Press, American Press, Association Press, 1966.

Abraham, K. C., ed. *Third World Theologies: Commonalities and Differences.* Maryknoll, NY: Orbis Books, 1990.

Anderson, Gerald H., ed. *The Theology of the Christian Mission.* New York: McGraw-Hill, 1961.

Anderson, Gerald H., and Thomas F. Stransky, eds. *Mission Trends No. 1, Crucial Issues in Mission Today.* New York: Paulist Press and Grand Rapids, MI: William B. Eerdmans Publishing Company, 1974.

Anderson, Gerald H., and Thomas F. Stransky, eds. *Mission Trends No. 5, Faith Meets Faith.* New York: Paulist Press and Grand Rapids, MI: William B. Eerdmans Publishing Company, 1981.

Anderson, Norman. *Christianity and World Religions, The Challenge of Pluralism.* Downer's Grove, IL: Inter-Varsity Press, 1984. (An enlarged and updated version of a 1970 edition with the title, *Christianity and Comparative Religion.*)

Ante-Nicene Fathers, Vol. 1. Grand Rapids, MI: William B. Eerdmans Publishing Company, 1953.

Barrett, David B., ed. *World Christian Encyclopedia.* New York: Oxford University Press, 1982.

Bible, The. The Revised Standard Version. Nashville, TN: Thomas Nelson Publishers, 1989.

Bouquet, A. C. "Revelation and the Divine Logos." In *The Theology of the Christian Mission*, ed. Gerald H. Anderson. New York: McGraw-Hill Book Company, 1961.

Brunner, Emil. *Revelation and Reason: The Christian Doctrine of Faith and Knowledge.* Tr. Olive Wyon. Philadelphia: Westminster Press, 1946.

Bulletin of the Pontifical Council on Interreligious Dialogue Vol. 26, No. 2. Rome: Vatican Polyglot Press, 1991.

Carter, John Ross. "Translational Theology: An Expression of Christian Faith in a Religiously Plural World." In *Christian Faith in a Religiously Plural World*, ed. Donald G. Dawe and John B. Carman. Maryknoll, NY: Orbis Books, 1980.

Cobb, John B., Jr. *Beyond Dialogue.* Philadelphia: Fortress Press, 1982.

———. "Beyond Pluralism." In *Christian Uniqueness Reconsidered: The Myth of a Pluralistic Theology of Religions,* ed. Gavin D'Costa. Maryknoll, NY: Orbis Books, 1990.

———. *Christ in a Pluralistic Age.* Philadelphia: Fortress Press, 1975.

Copeland, E. Luther. *Christianity and World Religions.* Nashville, TN: Convention Press, 1963.

———. *World Mission and World Survival.* Nashville, TN: Broadman Press, 1985.

Cragg, Kenneth. *Christ and the Faiths.* Philadelphia: Westminster Press, 1986.

Dawe, Donald G., and John B. Carman, eds. *Christian Faith in a Religiously Plural World.* Maryknoll, NY: Orbis Books, 1980.

D'Costa, Gavin. "Christ, the Trinity and Religious Plurality." In *Christian Uniqueness Reconsidered: The Myth of a Pluralistic Theology of Religions,* ed. Gavin D'Costa. Maryknoll, NY: Orbis Books, 1990.

———. *John Hick's Theology of Religions: A Critical Evaluation.* Lanham, MD: University Press of America, 1987.

———. *Theology and Religious Pluralism.* Oxford: Basil Blackwell, 1986.

———, ed. *Christian Uniqueness Reconsidered: The Myth of a Pluralistic Theology of Religions.* Maryknoll, NY: Orbis Books, 1990.

de Silva, Lynn. "Emergent Theology in the Context of Asia." In *Asian Christian Theology: Emerging Trends,* ed. Douglas L. Elwood. Philadelphia: The Westminster Press, 1980.

———. *The Problem of the Self in Buddhism and Christianity.* Colombo: Study Centre for Religion and Society, 1975.

———. *Reincarnation in Buddhist and Christian Thought.* Colombo: Christian Literature Society of Ceylon, 1968.

"Dialogue and Proclamation." *Bulletin of the Pontifical Council on Interreligious Dialogue,* Vol. 26, No. 2. Rome: Vatican Polyglot Press, 1991.

Driver, Tom. "The Case for Pluralism." In *The Myth of Christian Uniqueness: Toward a Pluralistic Theology of Religions,* ed. John Hick and Paul F. Knitter. Maryknoll, NY: Orbis Books, 1987.

Drummond, Richard Henry. *Toward a New Age in Christian Theology.* Maryknoll, NY: Orbis Books, 1985.

Dupuis, Jacques. *Toward a Christian Theology of Religious Pluralism.* Maryknoll, NY: Orbis Books, 1997.

Elwood, Douglas L., ed. *Asian Christian Theology: Emerging Trends.* Philadelphia: The Westminster Press, 1980.

Erickson, Millard J. "Hope for Those Who Haven't Heard? Yes, But . . . ." *Evangelical Missions Quarterly,* 11 (April 1975).

Evangelical Missions Quarterly, 11 (April 1975).

Fabella, Virginia, and Sun Ai Lee Park, eds. *We Dare to Dream: Doing Theology as Asian Women.* Hong Kong and Manila: Asian Women's Resource Center for Culture and Theology and The EATWOT Women's Commission in Asia, 1989.

Faber, Frederick W. "There's a Wideness in God's Mercy." In *The New Church Hymnal*, ed. H. Augustine Smith *et al.* New York: Fleming H. Revell Company, 1937.

Fernando, Ajith. *The Christian Attitude Toward World Religions.* Wheaton, IL: Tyndale House Publishers, 1987.

Freytag, Walter. *The Gospel and the Religions.* London: SCM Press, 1957.

Freud, Sigmund. *The Future of an Illusion.* W. B. Robson-Scott, ed. and tr. Garden City, NY: Doubleday and Company, 1964.

Gilkey, Langdon. "Plurality and Its Theological Implications." In *The Myth of Christian Uniqueness: Toward a Pluralistic Theology of Religions,* ed. John Hick and Paul F. Knitter. Maryknoll, NY: Orbis Books, 1987.

Hellwig, Monika. "Christology in the Wider Ecumenism." In *Christian Uniqueness Reconsidered: The Myth of a Pluralistic Theology of Religions,* ed. Gavin D'Costa. Maryknoll, NY: Orbis Books, 1990.

Hick, John. *A Christian Theology of Religions: The Rainbow of Faiths.* Louisville, KY: Westminster/John Knox Press, 1995.

——, and Brian Hebblethwaite, eds. *Christianity and Other Religions, Selected Readings.* Philadelphia: Fortress Press, 1980.

——, and Paul F. Knitter, eds. *The Myth of Christian Uniqueness: Toward a Pluralistic Theology of Religions.* Maryknoll, NY: Orbis Books, 1987.

———. "The Non-Absoluteness of Christianity." In *The Myth of Christian Uniqueness: Toward a Pluralistic Theology of Religions*, ed. John Hick and Paul F. Knitter. Maryknoll, NY: Orbis Books, 1987.

———. "Whatever Path Men Choose Is Mine." In *Christianity and Other Religions, Selected Readings*, ed. John Hick and Brian Hebblethwaite. Philadelphia: Fortress Press, 1980.

Hocking, William Ernest. *The Coming World Civilization*. New York: Harper and Brothers, 1956.

———. *Living Religions and a World Faith*. London: George Allen and Unwin, 1940.

———. Chairman, Commission of Appraisal. *Re-Thinking Missions: A Laymen's Inquiry After One Hundred Years*. New York: Harper and Brothers, 1932.

Howe, Reuel. *The Miracle of Dialogue*. New York: Seabury Press, 1963.

Imasogie, Isador. *Guidelines for Christian Theology in Africa*. Achimoto, Ghana: African Press, 1983.

International Bulletin of Missionary Research, Vol.15, No.2 (April 1991).

International Bulletin of Missionary Research, Vol.15, No.3 (July 1991).

Jaspers, Karl. *The Origin and Goal of History*. Michael Bullock, tr. London: Routledge and Kegan Paul, 1953.

Johnston, George, and Wolfgang Roth, eds. *The Church in the Modern World*. Toronto: The Ryerson Press, 1967.

Justin Martyr. *The First Apology of Justin. Ante-Nicene Fathers*, Vol. 1. Grand Rapids, MI: William B. Eerdmans Publishing Company, 1953.

———. *The Second Apology of Justin. Ante-Nicene Fathers*, Vol. 1. Grand Rapids, MI: William B. Eerdmans Publishing Company, 1953.

Kane, J. Herbert. *Understanding Christian Missions*. Grand Rapids, MI: Baker Book House, 1974.

Khodr, Georges. "The Economy of the Holy Spirit." In *Mission Trends No. 5, Faith Meets Faith*, ed. Gerald H. Anderson and Thomas F. Stransky. New York: Paulist Press, and Grand Rapids, MI: William B. Eerdmans Publishing Company, 1981.

———. "An Orthodox Perspective on Interreligious Dialogue." *Current Dialogue*, 19 (January 1991): 25-27"

Knitter, Paul F. "Catholic Theology of Religions at a Crossroads." In *Christianity among the Religions*, ed. Hans Küng and Jürgen Moltmann. Edinburgh: T & T Clark, 1986.

———. *Jesus and the Other Names: Christian Mission and Global Responsibility.* Maryknoll, NY: Orbis Books, 1996.

———. "Theocentric Christology." *Theology Today* 40 (July 1983).

———. "Toward a Liberation Theology of Religions." In *The Myth of Christian Uniqueness: Toward a Pluralistic Theology of Religions,* ed. John Hick and Paul F. Knitter. Maryknoll, NY: Orbis Press, 1987.

———, ed. *Pluralism and Oppression: Theology in World Perspective.* Lanham, MD: University Press of America, 1988.

Koyama, Kosuke. "What Makes a Missionary? Toward Crucified Mind, Not Crusading Mind." In *Mission Trends No. 1,* ed. Gerald H. Anderson and Thomas F. Stransky. New York: Paulist Press, and Grand Rapids, MI: William B. Eerdmans Publishing Company, 1974.

Kraemer, Hendrik. "Continuity or Discontinuity." *The Authority of the Faith, Madras Series,* Vol. 1. New York: International Missionary Council, 1939.

———. *The Christian Message in a Non-Christian World.* New York: Harper and Brothers, 1938.

———. *Religion and the Christian Faith.* London: Lutterworth Press, 1956.

———. *World Cultures and World Religions: The Coming Dialogue.* Philadelphia: The Westminster Press, 1960.

———. *Why Christianity of All Religions?* Philadelphia: The Westminster Press, 1962.

Küng, Hans. *On Being a Christian.* New York: Doubleday & Company Image Books, 1984.

———, and Jürgen Moltmann, eds. *Christianity Among the Religions.* Edinburgh: T & T Clark, 1986.

Lam, Wing-hung. *Chinese Theology in Construction.* Pasadena: William Carey Library, 1983.

Lapide, Pinchas, and Jürgen Moltmann. *Jewish Monotheism and Christian Trinitarian Doctrine.* Translated from the German by Leonard Swidler. Philadelphia: Fortress Press, 1981.

Lindsell, Harold. *An Evangelical Theology of Missions.* Grand Rapids, MI: Zondervan Publishing House, 1970. (A republication with no substantive change of *A Christian Philosophy of Missions.* Wheaton, IL: Van Kampen, 1949.)

Mackay, John A. *Ecumenics.* Englewood Cliffs, NJ: Prentice-Hall, 1964.

Majumdar, R. C., ed. *Swami Vivekananda Centenary Memorial Volume.* Calcutta: Swami Vivekananda Centenary, 1963.

McCarthy, Caritas."Christianity from an African Perspective." In *Pluralism and Oppression: Theology in World Perspective,* ed. Paul F. Knitter. Lanham, MD: University Press of America, 1988.

McGavran, Donald Anderson. *The Bridges of God: A Study in the Strategy of Missions.* London: World Dominion Press, 1957.

———. *Momentous Decisions in Missions Today.* Grand Rapids, MI: Baker Book House, 1984.

———. *Understanding Church Growth.* Grand Rapids, MI: William B. Eerdmans Publishing Company, 1970.

Moltmann, Jürgen. "Christianity and the World Religions." In *Christianity and Other Religions, Selected Readings,* ed. John Hick and Brian Hebblethwaite. Philadelphia: Fortress Press, 1980.

Netland, Harold A. *Dissonant Voices: Religious Pluralism and the Question of Truth.* Grand Rapids, MI: William B. Eerdmans Publishing Company, 1991.

Newbigin, Lesslie. "The Basis, Purpose and Manner of Inter-Faith Dialogue." In *Interreligious Dialogue: Facing the Next Frontier,* Vol. 1, ed. Richard W. Rousseau. Scranton, PA: Ridge Row Press, 1981.

———. *The Finality of Christ.* London: SCM Press, 1969.

———. *The Gospel in a Pluralist Society.* Grand Rapids, MI: William B. Eerdmans Publishing Company and Geneva: World Council of Churches Publications, 1989.

———. *The Open Secret: Sketches for a Missionary Theology.* Grand Rapids, MI: William B. Eerdmans Publishing Company, 1978.

———. "Religion for the Marketplace." In *Christian Uniqueness Reconsidered: The Myth of a Pluralistic Theology of Religions,* ed. Gavin D'Costa. Maryknoll, NY: Orbis Books, 1990.

———. *Trinitarian Faith and Today's Mission.* Richmond, VA: John Knox Press, 1964.

North, C. R. "Sacrifice." In *A Theological Wordbook of the Bible,* ed. Alan Richardson. New York: The Macmillan Company, 1950.

Oxtoby, Willard G., ed. *Religious Diversity: Essays of W. C. Smith.* New York: Harper and Row, 1976.

Panikkar, Raimondo (Raymond). "Can Theology Be Transcultural?" In *Pluralism and Oppression: Theology in World Perspective,* ed. Paul F. Knitter. Lanham, MD: University of America Press, 1991.

———. "The Jordan, the Tiber and the Ganges." In *The Myth of Christian Uniqueness: Toward a Pluralistic Theology of Religions,* ed. John Hick and Paul F. Knitter. Maryknoll, NY: Orbis Books, 1987.

——. *The Trinity and the Religious Experience of Man: Icon—Person—Mystery.* Maryknoll, NY: Orbis Books, and London: Darton, Longman and Todd, 1973.

——. *The Unknown Christ of Hinduism.* London: Darton, Longman and Todd, 1964.

Partain, Jackie Gene. "Themes in Contemporary African Theology." Th. D. Dissertation, Southwestern Baptist Theological Seminary, Fort Worth, TX, 1983.

Perry, Edmund. *The Gospel in Dispute.* Garden City, NY: Doubleday & Company, 1958.

Peters, Ted. *God as Trinity: Relationality and Temporality in Divine Life.* Louisville, KY: Westminster/John Knox Press, 1993.

Pieris, Aloysius. *An Asian Theology of Liberation.* Maryknoll, NY: Orbis Books, 1988.

——. "The Buddha and the Christ: Mediators of Liberation." In *The Myth of Christian Uniqueness: Toward a Pluralistic Theology of Religions,* ed. John Hick and Paul F. Knitter. Maryknoll, NY: Orbis Books, 1987.

——. *Love Meets Wisdom: A Christian Experience of Buddhism.* Maryknoll, NY: Orbis Books, 1988.

Pinnock, Clark. *A Wideness in God's Mercy: The Finality of Jesus Christ in a World of Religions.* Grand Rapids, MI: Zondervan Publishing House, 1992.

Race, Alan. *Christians and Religious Pluralism: Patterns in the Christian Theology of Religions.* Maryknoll, NY: Orbis Books, 1982.

Rahner, Karl. "Christianity and the Non-Christian Religions." In *Christianity and Other Religions, Selected Readings,* ed. John Hick and Brian Hebblethwaite. Philadelphia: Fortress Press, 1980.

Redemptor Missio. See extensive excerpts from this papal encyclical in *International Bulletin of Missionary Research* 15 (April 1991); and in James A. Scherer and Stephen B. Bevans, eds. *New Directions in Mission and Evangelization 1: Basic Statements 1974-1991.* Maryknoll, NY: Orbis Books, 1992.

Reuther, Rosemary. "Feminism and Jewish-Christian Dialogue." In *The Myth of Christian Uniqueness: Toward a Pluralistic Theology of Religions,* ed. John Hick and Paul F. Knitter. Maryknoll, NY: Orbis Books, 1987.

Richardson, Alan. *A Theological Wordbook of the Bible.* New York: The Macmillan Company, 1950.

Richardson, Don. *Eternity in Their Hearts.* Revised edition. Ventura, CA: Regal Books, 1981.

Rolfe, William J., ed. *Tennyson's In Memoriam.* Boston: Houghton Mifflin & Company, 1895.

Rouner, Leroy. "Theology of Religions in Recent Protestant Theology." In *Christianity among the Religions,* ed. Hans Küng and Jürgen Moltmann Edinburgh: T & T Clark, 1986.

Rowley, H. H. *The Biblical Doctrine of Election.* London: Lutterworth Press, 1950.

Samartha, S[tanley]. J. *Courage for Dialogue: Ecumenical Issues in Inter-Religious Relationships.* Geneva: World Council of Churches, 1981.

─────. "The Cross and the Rainbow: Christ in a Multireligious Culture." In *The Myth of Christian Uniqueness: Toward a Pluralistic Theology of Religions.,* ed. John Hick and Paul F. Knitter. Maryknoll, NY: Orbis Books, 1987.

─────, ed. *Living Faiths and the Ecumenical Movement.* Geneva: World Council of Churches, 1971.

─────. *One Christ—Many Religions: Toward a Revised Christology.* Maryknoll, NY: Orbis Books, 1991.

Scherer, James, and Stephen B. Bevans, eds. *New Directions in Missions and Evangelization 1: Basic Statements 1974-1991.* Maryknoll, NY: Orbis Books, 1992.

Schlette, Heinz Robert. *Towards a Theology of Religions.* New York: Herder and Herder, 1966.

Smith, Wilfred Cantwell. "The Future of the Church and the Future of Mission." In *The Church in the Modern World,* ed. George Johnston and Wolfgang Rolf. Toronto: The Ryerson Press, 1967.

─────. "Participation: The Changing Christian Role in Other Cultures." In *Religious Diversity: Essays of W. C. Smith,* ed. Willard G. Oxtoby. New York: Harper and Row, 1976.

─────. *Towards a World Theology: Faith and the Comparative History of Religions.* Philadelphia: The Westminster Press, 1981.

Sobrino, Jon. "Theology in a Suffering World: Theology as *Intellectus Amoris.*" In *Pluralism and Oppression: Theology in World Perspective,* ed. Paul F. Knitter. Lanham, MD: University Press of America, 1988.

Song, Choan-Seng. *Christian Mission in Reconstruction—An Asian Analysis.* Maryknoll, NY: Orbis Books, 1977.

─────. *Third-Eye Theology: Theology in Asian Settings.* Maryknoll, NY: Orbis Books, 1979.

Spielberg, Fana, and Stuart Dauermann. "Contextualization: Witness and Reflection, Messianic Jews as a Case." *Missiology*, 25 (January, 1997): 15-30.

Stewart, James S. *Thine Is the Kingdom*. New York: Charles Scribner's Sons, 1956.

Suchocki, Marjorie. "In Search of Justice." In *The Myth of Christian Uniqueness: Toward a Pluralistic Theology of Religions*, ed. John Hick and Paul F. Knitter. Maryknoll, NY: Orbis Books, 1987.

Taylor, John V. *The Go-Between God: The Holy Spirit and the Christian Mission*. Philadelphia: Fortress Press, 1973.

———. *The Primal Vision*. Philadelphia: Fortress Press, 1963.

———. "The Theological Basis of Interfaith Dialogue." In *Christianity and Other Religions, Selected Readings*, ed. John Hick and Brian Hebblethwaite. Philadelphia: Fortress Press, 1980.

Tennyson, Alfred Lord. "In Memoriam." William J. Rolfe, ed. *Tennyson's In Memoriam*. Boston: Houghton Mifflin & Company, 1895.

Tillich, Paul. *Christianity and the Encounter of the World Religions*. New York: Columbia University Press, 1963.

———. *Dynamics of Faith*. New York: Harper and Brothers, 1957.

———. *Systematic Theology*, 3 Vols. Chicago: University of Chicago Press, 1951, 1957, 1963.

Toynbee, Arnold. "Encounters Between Civilizations." In *Civilization on Trial*. New York: Oxford University Press, 1969. (First published in *Harper's Magazine*, April, 1947.)

———. *Experiences*. New York: Oxford University Press, 1969.

Vanhoozer, Kevin J., ed. *The Trinity in a Pluralistic Age*. Grand Rapids, MI: William B. Eerdmans Publishing Company, 1977.

Vivekananda, Swami. *Swami Vivekananda Centenary Memorial Volume*. R. C. Majumdar, ed. Calcutta: Swami Vivekananda Centenary, 1963.

Warren, M. A. C. General Introduction to *The Primal Vision*, by John V. Taylor. Philadelphia: Fortress Press, 1963.

Williams, Rowan. "Trinity and Pluralism." In *Christian Uniqueness Reconsidered: The Myth of a Pluralistic Theology of Religions*, ed. Gavin D'Costa. Maryknoll, NY: Orbis Books, 1990.

World Council of Churches, *Dialogue with People of Living Faiths*. Geneva: World Council of Churches, 1981.

———. *Guidelines on Dialogue with People of Living Faiths and Ideologies*. Geneva: World Council of Churches, 1979.

INDEX

Abraham, 53, 64, 65, 68, 113, 116
absolute(s), 9, 15, 16, 35, 102, 139
Africa, 4, 10, 11, 12, 13, 18, 98, 106
African Americans, 11
agnostic, 66, 67, 132, 133, 143
Anderson, Norman, 38–39, 60
Anglican, 34, 37, 38, 102, 133
annihilationism, 67, 70, 71
anonymous Christians, 123, 125
Antioch, 35
Apostles' Creed, 68
apostles, 80, 113, 114
Aristotelianism, 3
ascesis, 28
Asia, Asians, 4, 10, 11, 12, 13, 18, 26, 27, 28, 38, 98, 106, 107, 129, 133, 138
Asian liberation theology, 12, 26
Asmat, 61
atheists, 132, 140
Axial Period, 24, 128

Baha'i, 93, 118, 119, 135
Balaam, 63
Banaras, 77
Baptist, 44, 107, 109
Barnabas, 54
Barth, Karl, 7, 21, 51, 61
Belgian, 31
biosphere, 27
body of Christ, 121
Book of Revelation, 65
Bouquet, A. C., 56
Brahman, 36
bride of Christ, 121
Brunner, Emil, 7, 51, 64
Buddha, 14, 28, 100
Buddhism, Buddhist(s), 12, 26–28, 36–40, 57, 69, 78, 79, 92, 93, 100, 102, 104, 106, 109, 112, 129, 135, 138, 139
Burmese Bible, 13

Cabazilas, Nicholas, 36
Carey, William, 86
categories, 73, 130, 143, 144

China, Chinese, 13, 20, 85, 91
"chosenness", 126, 128
Christ, 105, 106
Christian Councils, 21
Christian theology, viii, 5
Christian, 99, 110, 126
christocentric pluralism, 9, 30, 56
christocentrism, 25, 30, 40
Christology, Christological, 21, 25, 26, 27, 28, 29, 30, 31, 32, 33, 39, 41, 45, 55, 99
church growth, 83, 84, 118
Church of South India, 30
church, 113, 122, 123, 124, 125, 126, 135
city of God, 104, 121, 139, 140
Clement of Alexandria, 61
clues, 50, 54, 55, 57, 129
Cobb, John B., Jr., 25, 29, 37, 39, 40, 52
colonialism, 17, 18, 19, 20, 77, 85, 99
common essence, 51, 52, 61
communication, 4, 81, 83, 85, 106, 124, 143
Communist, 85
community, 121, 122, 123, 124, 125, 139, 140
comparative religion, 5, 14
confessionalism, 9, 81, 82
conservative, 67, 95, 114
contextualization, 87, 104, 106
convergences, 115
conversion, 105, 115
Copernican revolution, 23, 41
cosmic, 55, 56, 70, 71, 72, 76, 130
Cragg, Kenneth, 34, 37, 38
creation, 57, 76, 129, 130, 140
creativity, 57, 59, 60
creator, 55, 62, 71

cross, 70, 75, 83, 102, 139
"cross-reference" theology, 37, 38
Crusades, 118
Cullmann, Oscar, 30
cultural imperialism, 17
cultural renascence, 18
culture, 38, 42, 52, 60–63, 69, 77, 80, 85, 87, 90, 104, 105, 108, 114, 122, 128, 130, 131, 133, 134, 135, 144

D'Costa, Gavin, ix, 34, 35, 54
Dalai Lama, 112
Dao, 12, 57
Darwinism, vii, 3
deism, 14
deity, 100, 111, 117
demon(ic), 39, 58, 59, 143
demonic deception, 57, 58, 60
Dharma (Dhamma), 12, 57
dialecticism, 9, 80
dialogical, 42, 81, 84, 85, 91, 99, 106
discontinuity, 60, 61
divine, 14, 39, 41, 54, 59, 60, 62, 144
Dulles, Avery, 25
Dupuis, Jacques, ix, 23, 31–34, 143

East Asian, 100
ecumenical, ecumenism, 12, 17, 40, 73, 59, 82, 87, 110, 111, 123
ecclesiocentrism, 25
Egypt, 38
Enlightenment, 14–18
environment, 30, 90, 92, 110, 125
Ephesians, 70
Epiphany, 37
eschatology, 33, 36, 37, 40, 45, 51, 121, 122, 125, 138, 139, 143

eschaton, 10, 28, 125, 144
ethical, ethics, 19, 42, 53, 63, 67, 87, 88, 89, 105, 108, 125, 144
Europe, 92
evangelical, evangelicalism, 44, 46
evangelism, 45, 50, 86, 88, 90, 98, 102, 103, 104, 105, 106, 114, 118
evil, 58, 59, 65, 72, 75, 77, 82
evolution, 16, 27
exclusivism, exclusivist(s), vii, 6, 7, 8, 25, 27, 28, 30, 34, 35, 37, 114, 126, 127

Faber, Frederick, 46
faith, 72, 73, 75, 77, 81, 82, 84, 85, 89, 92, 94, 100–108, 110, 111, 113, 116, 130, 133–137, 140, 141, 144
Father, 74, 91, 113, 114, 131
fellowship, 121, 122, 145
Fernando, Ajith, 43, 44, 64
fideism, 82, 144
Freud, Sigmund, 131, 132
Freytag, Walter, 42
frontier peoples, 87
future of religion, 134

Gandhi, Mohandas, 62
Ganges, 20
Gautama, 28
Genesis, 16
Gentile(s), 43, 64, 65, 70, 80, 113, 114, 115, 116, 122
German, 114
Gilkey, Langdon, 17, 52, 59
glory of God, 139, 140
God's new order, 9, 124, 125
Golden Rule, 19, 94
grace, 66, 68, 69, 72, 75

Great Ancestor, 13
Great Britain, 40
Greco-Roman world, 3
Greece, Greek, 13, 21, 30, 38, 57, 110, 117
Greek Orthodox, 35

Hebrew, Hebrews, 64, 67, 68, 70, 113, 121
Heilsgeschichte, 126, 129
hell, 66, 67
Hellenized, 117
Hellwig, Monika, 140
Heraclitus, 56
Herberg, Will, 114
hermeneutical theology, 32
Hick, John, 23–24, 27, 29, 31, 33, 34, 40, 41, 43, 46
Hindu, Hinduism, 13, 19, 20, 28, 29, 30, 33, 37, 77, 44, 57, 69, 86, 102, 104, 106, 108, 133, 134, 135, 138
history of religions, 128
Hocking, William Ernest, 66, 67, 135, 136, 137
Holy Spirit, 35, 36, 54, 59, 74, 81, 83, 85, 91, 105, 117
homophobia, 58
homosexuals, 11
Howe, Reuel, 99
humility, 18, 44, 77, 79, 81, 91, 109, 118, 144
hypostasis, 117

ideal, 108, 121, 122, 123
imagination, 59
imperialism, 77, 81, 99, 106, 109, 134
incarnate, incarnation, 9, 22, 24, 30, 33, 36, 39, 40, 45, 53, 56, 70, 75, 79, 80, 81, 91, 117,

INCARNATE, INCARNATION
(continued)
    118, 128, 129, 130, 135
inclusivism, viii, 6, 8, 25, 27, 28, 30, 34, 37, 53
India, Indian, 13, 19, 20, 30, 31, 34, 40, 44, 73, 77, 91, 98, 108, 118
indigenization, 87, 104, 106
inerrancy, 43, 52
institution, 121, 122, 123, 125
interfaithism, 111
International Missionary Council, 61, 98
interreligious cooperation, 82, 91, 106, 107, 110, 111
interreligious dialogue, 97–101, 104, 106, 111, 112
interreligious relationships, vii, 37, 50, 82, 97, 111, 119
interreligious worship, 97, 111, 112
Iran, 119
Ireneaus, 33
Ishvara, 13
Islam, Islamic, 37, 38, 93, 104, 113, 116, 117, 118, 135, 138
Israel, Israelites, 63, 64, 70, 71, 113, 116, 126, 127

Jain(s), Jainism, 104, 108, 109
Japan, Japanese, 13, 78, 92
Jerusalem, 83
Jesuit, 31
Jesus, 30, 90, 91, 93, 102, 103, 105, 111, 113, 114, 115, 117, 118
Jewish monotheism, 21
Jews, Judaism, 17, 37, 38, 68, 70, 83, 94, 103, 104, 107, 111, 113, 114, 115, 116, 117, 118, 123, 124, 126
Job, 64
John Birch Society, 123
Judaizers, 122
judgment, 44, 54, 65, 66, 67, 68, 69, 82
justice, 71, 76, 85, 107, 129
Justin Martyr, 36, 56

karma, 19
kenosis, 42
Khodr, Georges, 35-37
kingdom of God, 76
kingdomcentric (soteriocentric) pluralism, 25
Knitter, Paul, ix, 23–25, 27, 29, 33, 34, 35, 40, 43, 46, 73, 81
Korea, 12
Kosuke Koyama, 79
Kraemer, Hendrik, 7, 51, 60, 61, 80, 98
Küng, Hans, 25, 110

latent church, 84, 123, 125
Latin America, 10, 11, 12, 13
Latin, 13, 117
liberation theology, 11, 25, 26
Lindsell, Harold, 64
Logos, 9, 12, 29, 30, 33, 36, 38, 41, 45, 54, 55, 56, 57, 60, 61, 72, 75, 130
Lord, 10, 21, 31, 53, 59, 76, 79, 90, 91, 93, 105, 144
love, 17, 26, 35, 36, 52, 66, 68, 69, 74, 76, 84, 85, 89, 106, 130
Luther, Martin, 52

Mackay, John, 80
Madras, India, 61
Malachi, 65

McGavran, Donald A., 83, 84
Melchizedek, 64
Messiah, 111, 115, 117
Messianic Jews, 114
Methodism, Methodist(s), 39, 109
Minjung theology, 12
missiology, 37, 40, 42, 83, 88, 90
mission(s), missionary, missionaries, vii, 43, 45, 50, 64, 72–94, 97, 104, 105, 106, 114, 115, 116, 118, 124, 128, 129, 145
missionary earthkeeper, 90
Moltmann, Jürgen, 89, 115, 116
monological, 81, 106
monotheism, monotheistic, 14, 21, 30, 31, 50, 111, 113, 116, 117, 118, 131
Mosaic law, 53
Muhammad, 116, 117, 118
Muslim, 36, 69, 83, 85, 86, 103, 106, 107, 109, 111, 116, 117, 118

Nagasaki, 92
Native Americans, 11, 83, 108
negativism, 8
New Guinea, 61
Newbigin, Lesslie, 8, 40, 41, 42, 43, 60, 101, 102, 103
Nirvana, 100
Noah, 65
non-professional missionaries, 88
non-relativistic pluralism, 10
nonresidential missionaries, 88, 89
noösphere, 27

O'Leary, J. S., 33

Pacific Islands, 10
Palestine, 38

Panikkar, Raimundo (Raymond), 20, 23, 28-30, 52
paradoxical pluralism, 9
Parseeism, 118
passive resistance, 62
Paul, 54, 59, 75, 79, 80, 91, 113, 114, 122
Pentecost, 122
Pentecostalism, 126
Persia, 91, 118
Pieris, Aloysius, 12, 23, 26–28, 33, 34, 124, 125
Pinnock, Clark H., ix, 16, 17, 44, 45, 46, 66
pluralism, viii, 6, 8, 10, 11, 13, 14, 15, 18–23, 25–34, 40, 43, 45, 46, 94, 139, 143
polytheism, 117
pre-Constantinian, 118
pre-eschatological agnoticism, 10
Presbyterianism, 23
prophet(s), 56, 113, 116, 117, 126, 127
proselytism, 105
Protestant Reformation, 126
Protestant, 17, 125
Ptolemaic conception, 23

Qur'an, 14, 116, 117

Race, Alan, 7
radical displacement, 136, 137
Rahner, Karl, 46, 123, 124
Ramakrishna Mission, 108
reason, 57
reconception, 135–138
redeemed community, 121
redemptive events, 129, 130
relational Christology, 32
relativism, 13, 15, 16, 18, 20, 21, 26, 34, 84, 98, 99, 110, 111
religious freedom, 107, 108

religious history, 130
Renaissance, 14
revelation, 13–15, 21, 22, 36, 38, 39, 41, 43, 44, 50–52, 54–58, 60–62, 64, 65, 73–75, 82, 100, 118, 121, 124, 128, 130, 143, 144
revelational norm, 50
revelational ultimacy, 20
Richardson, Don, 61, 64
Roman Catholicism, Roman Catholic(s), 17, 24, 26, 28, 29, 31, 34, 39, 46, 124, 125
Rome, Roman(s), 31, 38, 59, 107
Rosenzweig, Franz, 114, 115

sacraments, 39, 69
sacred history, 128
sacrifice, 70, 71, 72, 86, 102
sages, 56
salvation history, 126, 127, 128, 129, 130
salvation, 36, 37, 38, 41, 42, 44, 45, 50, 51, 62, 63, 64, 65, 66, 68, 69, 70, 71, 72, 74, 75, 76, 100, 102, 116, 123, 125, 126, 139, 144
salvific events, 129
Samartha, Stanley J., 23, 30, 31, 33, 73, 93, 94, 98, 110, 127
Satan, 58
Savior, 10, 21, 31, 32
Schlette, H. R., 130
scientific movement, 16
Scriptures, 52, 53, 62, 63, 67, 68, 74, 78, 113, 117
secular, secularism, secularization, 18, 122, 123, 131
Semitic, Semiticization, 116, 117, 118
Shi'ite Islam, 118

Shinto, 104
Sikhism, Sikhs, 104, 118
Smith, Wilfred Cantwell, ix, 29, 76, 89, 93, 128, 130
Sobrino, Jon, 11
Socrates, 56
Song, Choan-Seng, 85, 107, 129, 130
soteriology, 9, 25, 26, 30
South Asian, 100
South India, 77
Spain, 28
Spiritual Community, 123, 124
Sri Lanka, Sri Lankan, 12, 13, 26, 43, 124
Stewart, James S., 74
syncretism, 37, 98, 103, 104, 136, 138
Synoptic Gospels, 55
synthesis, 136, 137

Taylor, John V., 55, 102, 103
theistic, 30
theocentric pluralism, 9
theocentrism, 25, 40
theological questions, 5
theology of religion(s), vii, 5, 53, 82, 83, 87, 90, 143
Theravada Buddhism, 24, 100
Third World Christians, 90
Third World churches, 90
Third World missionaries, 90
Third World, 10, 11, 12, 13, 18, 27
Tillich, Paul, 5, 58, 66, 67, 84, 122, 124
Toynbee, Arnold J., 133, 134
Trinitarianism, 34, 41
Trinity, 21, 29, 30, 31, 33, 35, 36, 45, 54, 55, 99, 117
tritheism, 117
triumphalism, 45

Troeltsch, Ernst, 24

unevangelized, 88
ungospelized, 88
unitive pluralism, 25
unity, 82, 110, 134, 135
universal lordship, 91
universal, 72, 74, 75, 82, 94, 102, 104, 110, 124, 126, 128, 132, 139, 144
universe, 71, 76, 84, 105, 121, 122, 125, 140
unreached peoples, 87, 88

Varnasi, 77
Vatican II, 17, 32
Vatican, 26
Vivekananda, 108

Warren, M. A. C., 4, 100
Williams, Rowan, 29
witness, 103, 106, 107, 108, 114, 115, 116, 125, 136, 137
women, 11
Word, 41, 44
World Council of Churches, 98, 103, 110
world history, 128, 135
World Parliament of Religions of 1893, 98
world religions, 98, 110, 128

Yahweh, 126

Zoroastrianism, 118

www.ingramcontent.com/pod-product-compliance
Lightning Source LLC
Chambersburg PA
CBHW021830300426
44114CB00009BA/388